The Network Organization

NEW DIMENSIONS IN NETWORKS

Series Editor: Anna Nagurney, *John F. Smith Memorial Professor, Isenberg School of Management, University of Massachusetts at Amherst, USA*

Networks provide a unifying framework for conceptualizing and studying problems and applications. They range from transportation and telecommunication networks and logistic networks to economic, social and financial networks. This series is designed to publish original manuscripts and edited volumes that push the development of theory and applications of networks to new dimensions. It is interdisciplinary and international in its coverage, and aims to connect existing areas, unveil new applications and extend existing conceptual frameworks as well as methodologies. An outstanding editorial advisory board made up of scholars from many fields and many countries assures the high quality and originality of all of the volumes in the series.

Titles in the series include:

The Network Organization

The Experience of Leading French Multinationals

Emmanuel Josserand

University of Technology, Sydney
Université Paris Dauphine

NEW DIMENSIONS IN NETWORKS

Edward Elgar
Cheltenham, UK • Northampton, MA, USA

Published by
Edward Elgar Publishing Limited
Glensanda House
Montpellier Parade
Cheltenham
Glos GL50 1UA
UK

Edward Elgar Publishing, Inc.
136 West Street
Suite 202
Northampton
Massachusetts 01060
USA

A catalogue record for this book
is available from the British Library

ISBN 1 84376 594 2

Printed and bound in Great Britain by MPG Books Ltd, Bodmin, Cornwall

Contents

Figures

Tables

Acknowledgements

My gratitude goes first to Alain Dupont, CEO of Colas, who generously established a grant to finance the translation of this book into English. He thus confirmed the constant support he showed for this research, which started with completely free access to his company. This book owes a lot to him personally but also to all the personnel of Colas, the first case study.

Hervé Reumont (CFDP), Eric Nodet-Langlois (Air Liquide) and Jacques Dussart (GTIE) were also very supportive and patient in answering my time-consuming and detailed questions and requests.

I thank Bernard de Montmorillon and Thomas Clarke who encouraged me with indulgence in the process of publication.

Carlo Jarillo accepted to write a foreword to this English edition and I am very honored.

I don't know how I will ever be able to show enough gratitude to Judith Marquand for the incredible work she did on the English edition. She illuminated the text with her perfect English and was nice enough to say that she found an interest in doing so.

I also acknowledge the work done by Greg Joye and his collaborative translator Paul D. Nelson for translating this sometimes-difficult text.

The translation of this book was made possible thanks to a grant by Colas.

Preface by Bernard de Montmorillon

Throughout the first three quarters of the twentieth century, company executives, whether they were known as entrepreneurs or managers, benefited from a model of competitiveness that was both firmly validated and relatively simple. The neoclassical effort at formalism stressed the essential role of controlling costs in a competitive environment principally concerning relatively homogenized products. Within this same movement, the brilliant contributions of Frederick W. Taylor and Henri Fayol produced an analysis of the industrial company that was based on the division of labor and the primacy of hierarchy, which enabled them to propose organizational mechanisms that are essential to the control of costs as an efficient solution.

The Austrian marginalists, like the American and the French engineer, founded their recommendations on observation of the economic dynamic that prevailed at the end of the nineteenth century and up until World War I: innovation, mechanization, standardization, and wide distribution. The same general pattern can be found, magnified and internationalized, during the years of immense growth following World War II. Because of the competition among engineers with revitalized skills and the activity of reasonably motivated salespeople, company executives could rely on analogous rules to ensure growth, profit and peace in society founded on sharing the wealth which had thus been generated.

This dominant model of managerial efficiency has had its day. That is not to say that it is no longer representative. Entire areas of the global economy still lack, for the most part, the standard goods that have changed the lives of Westerners. At the same time, even the tertiary sector is experiencing a standardization which can still be explained by the Fordian model. Yet the unstoppable rise of service transactions in Western countries has put managers into new situations of uncertainty and forces them to call into question the model which has inspired as well as reassured them for so long.

Indeed, in a world of service transactions, competitiveness no longer raises the simple question of controlling costs. It imposes a direct, almost personal relationship with the client: it is no longer just about conceiving, manufacturing, stocking and distributing products that meet the customer's expectations. It now requires the development of a service relationship with the client, one in which he wants to be involved. This relationship is both complex and specific, and its material support is now only one element of support among many others which may be long-term, financial, educational, psychological, social – in other words intangible. In this context, the division of productive labor together with enlightened hierarchical management no longer offer reliable guidelines for ensuring profitability. Other processes need to be put into place, and managers are looking for new models which will allow them to gain control of the risks associated with the turbulence and the complexity of their environment. These two qualifiers, used to such an extent that it makes one smile, convey the difficulty of the task of today's entrepreneur: the service relationships they must manage are, by their very nature, heterogeneous (every client asks to be offered a distinctive service) and potentially unstable (every client is constantly solicited by other competitors). The organization must be able to respond to this heterogeneity and instability.

It is precisely at this point that Emmanuel Josserand's work is positioned. 'Industrial sectors,' he tells us from the beginning of his work, 'are evolving and comprise more and more customized services. Indeed, all sectors are converging towards a network mode of organization, centered around flexibility, including learning organizations which are capable of changing and resolving problems with the help of self-organized, coordinated, and interconnected processes.' The central and essential theme of Josserand's work lies in this concept. The network mode of organization is a pertinent response to the new conditions of competitiveness and not a form of competitiveness in and of itself, but by the process it conceals, the possibilities it creates, and the collective dynamic of service that it puts forth. The network, as Emmanuel Josserand has demonstrated and proven, is a logic of organization, in the active sense of the word, which responds to the present technical and social transformations.

The author's argument passes through several steps, following a logical progression that gives this work its power and clarity. First, we discover the concrete processes which make the network a method of organization that is able to give rise to the processes and behaviors necessary for rendering successful service. The analysis of the mechanisms of innovation in contact with the client, the description of the potential of transfers between units or teams, and the emphasis on the cohesion of the network not by means of hierarchical pressure but as an emerging collective project – all these introduce a renewed vision of the company in which the initiative is no longer decentralized or delegated, but is organized by the action of these peripheral entities. The author thus comes naturally to ask what is the role of the center from this perspective. Far from minimizing its importance, the author shows that this role is essential as a support to the transactions from which the network emerges as a factor of organizational cohesion. It is here that the author reaches the third level of his argument, which appears falsely paradoxical. The 'community of peripheral units,' which he reveals to us and which result from a networked organization, has invented a new mode of cohesion. This mode of cohesion yields a valuable, human, and creative organization linking together internal exchange, relevant corporate culture and hierarchy of an appropriate managerial logic.

The analysis proposed here, which must be studied in detail in order to appreciate its pertinence, has come at a perfect point. With the perspective gained from the passage of time, the author has been able to distance himself from the crises and organizational trends that have proliferated for the last twenty years. His approach is that of an involved researcher who is enriched by conceptual and theoretical reflection and who is constantly tackling issues in the field, as is shown by the four in-depth investigations that feed and enlighten the progress of his argument. This work illustrates the fertile and healthy renewal of the link between research and the company. As of late, management has become aware of the vital necessity of drawing on research. For the author, this forward-looking and creative approach no longer pertains only to pure science, but also, and perhaps primarily, to the humanities and social sciences. Emmanuel Josserand has positioned himself at this very crossroads.

Bernard de Montmorillon
President of the University of Paris-IX Dauphine

Foreword by Carlo Jarillo

'Organizational form' must come across as a fairly abstract concept. But it is an important one. Human beings have developed over the centuries ways to work together to accomplish tasks that could not be finished by a single person. In a way, organizations that coordinate the work of thousands of individuals, something we take for granted in our daily lives, are mankind's truly magnificent triumph: all other successes, be they technological, economic or social, depend crucially on that fusion of effort that complex organizations afford. Understanding how they work is, then, a precondition to understanding how mankind advances.

The story of that understanding is one of uncovering successive layers of complexity. The first organizational thinkers described the organizations as relatively simple artifacts, endowed with clear, overriding goals, simple lines of command, and uncomplicated sub-organizations. Armies were thus seen as examples, as was the Catholic Church or, more generally, what became known as 'bureaucracies.' That simplicity was supposed to be not just an empirical description, but a strong normative suggestion of how successful organizations should be run.

But organizations were not really that simple: it was their description that was so. Over the years, as organization scholars turned to patently more complex objects, such as multinational companies, it became evident that the simple rules that had been 'uncovered' for the proper management of a large organization could not account for the now evident complexity: successful organizations were clearly doing things against the best advice of the classical thinkers. Thus more sophisticated visions of what in fact was going on inside those organizations came to light, from 'M-forms' to 'matrices,' passing through 'ad-hocracies.' These added layers of complexity to the earlier models, and recognized that there is no one single organizational form, but many different ones.

Eventually, the very concept of 'organization' as an entity clearly separated from its environment became insufficient to describe what in reality goes on in many economic and social exchanges, and the concept of 'network' was introduced. This allowed a fresh look at complex organizations, made up of fairly differentiated sub-units, as well as the rich interactions that in fact make up the economic and social life of many geographic areas and industries, where small entities, formally independent, work together to produce substantial results. Thus from a fairly simple, vertical view of organizations, in which formal authority is the main coordinating mechanism, we came to see organizations in a more horizontal way, where trust and informal authority become the essential organizational principles. The last twenty years have seen the development and formalization of a body of knowledge of this new kind of organization, to which Professor Josserand's book is one of the latest additions.

But, somewhat contrary to frequent statements, including some in this book, I do not think that network organizations are in any way a new organizational form. More than a historical advance from simple, hierarchical, one-dimensional organizations towards ever more complex forms, what we have is a deepening of our understanding of a reality which was, to a very large extent, already there. Thus more than 'new organizational forms' what we have is 'new models' of how organizations work.

And having ever better models of how organizations work is essential. Even if organizations are never really 'designed' in their entirety, and develop by trial and error, without a clear architect, they must be managed. Understanding how they work, in all their richness, can only help us achieve our aims more efficiently, economic and socially. Professor Josserand's book is an important contribution to this understanding, in that it gets into the detail of how these complex network organizations actually work, precisely at their most difficult: it concentrates on the relationships among the peripheral units, and between those units and the center. This is precisely the essence of what *organization* is. By providing detailed empirical analysis built on a solid theoretical base, this book advances our ability to conceptualize and then manage the ever increasing complexity of those fascinating adventures that consist of harnessing the efforts of thousands of proudly independent individuals to the achievement of goals that exceed their abilities and enhance their lives, and that we call organizations.

JC Jarillo HEC
Université de Genève

1. Introducing the network organization

The horizontal organization chart, the myth of the inverted pyramid, the need to be customer-focused: such managerial recipes, abundant since the middle of the 1980s, have incited organizations to rethink their operations to increase flexibility and adaptability. Different modes have followed one after the other, all indicating that companies must change. This is clearly the major issue for a competitiveness that no longer resides in all-powerful strategic planning, but in flexibility and a certain organizational agility. Only this can bring about true proactiveness. Organizational change thus becomes the motor of strategy; the organization is no longer a constraint with which to deal. The grand schemes are finished. In their place are great changes − even the Army Management in France (Direction Générale des Armées) has adopted a structure much closer to the network company than to the linear hierarchy often associated with military organizations.

Fifteen or twenty years have passed during which avant-garde organizations in all sectors have realized the necessity for this fundamental mutation and its implications. Some of these organizations are simply in the process of beginning their revolution. Other more advanced ones have already successfully completed theirs. These revolutions do not simply concern the sectors of the New Economy, but older, more industrial and more stable sectors as well. Industrial activity evolves and demands more and more customized service. To accomplish this, all sectors are moving towards a networked organization, centered on flexibility, including learning organizations, which are capable of changing and of resolving problems by self-organized, self-coordinated and interconnected processes. Organizationally speaking, there are and will be fewer and fewer differences between the champions of the New Economy and older industrial juggernauts which will henceforth have broken their old mold or mutated.

Thus, we find ourselves at an important turning point, a moment where one can make a real assessment and evaluate the mutations of the pioneers of the network company. It means acknowledging the evolution and then analyzing the contents of this evolution in detail. This assessment must go beyond a mere 'cookbook' approach. Of course, it is necessary to show how much is at stake and to emphasize the need for evolution that is at the heart of the company's competitiveness. At the same time, the difficulties of this approach must not be forgotten, as is so often the case. This assessment must therefore be realistic and should highlight all the problems and traps that have shown up during recent transformations.

In particular, this emergence of new organizational forms makes obsolete the archetypal vision which claims that organizational cohesion can only rest on antagonistic relations between center and periphery. Organizational equilibrium is thus disturbed; the hierarchic skeleton, the foundation of cohesiveness in the majority of organizations, is shaken. In hierarchical cohesion, it is the center that is the keystone of the organizational edifice. It assures equilibrium by the pressure which it exerts on the periphery. It is this stability that is being questioned by these 'new' approaches. A new equilibrium has to be found in which the keystone no longer plays the same role. The periphery of the company now finds itself at the heart of the company's cohesion. The network spins its web and, as in modern architecture, the lightened structure does not necessarily thereby fall down. The cohesion of the network structure is therefore the product of a subtle balance between the central influence and relations between peripheral units. Before, these units did not play a recognizable central role, but now they must assure the cohesion of the organization. The transition concerns the relationship between center and periphery. The essential question which then arises concerns the cohesion of organizations where the center voluntarily reduces its influence, even to the point of disappearing completely in certain cases. How then does the integration of autonomous differentiated units happen? The investigation of the cohesion of the network company is at the heart of this book.

WHY CHANGE THE ORGANIZATION?

The arrival of 'new organizational forms,' linked with major mutations in companies' environments, calls into question the cohesion achieved through hierarchy. Before discussing our core question, that of cohesion, let us briefly consider those factors that have rendered this evolution necessary as well as those that have allowed this evolution to emerge.

The majority of publications on the theme of 'new organizational forms' or the networked company limit themselves merely to insisting that 'the world is more complex; there is a special form of turbulence in our time'. This gives the impression that there is a broad consensus, if not on the nature of new organizational forms, then at least on the factors that have prompted their emergence. The special features of a turbulence that may not correspond only to *our* time[1] must be put into perspective. We certainly minimize the importance of the two oil crises or other more recent economic crises if we compare them to the Stock Market crash of 1929. There is instead a return to a normal situation of turbulence that contrasts with the period of great stability of the *Trente Glorieuses*.[2] Nevertheless, even if the evolution of the organizational environment is no more unpredictable than it was at the beginning of the twentieth century, a certain number of elements have changed that have, in turn, pushed companies out of their bureaucratic shells. Indeed if, under certain conditions, competing companies abandon the stability assured by strategic planning, then there is no other solution than to rethink this process. As long as all the companies in one sector maintain a rigid planning system and as long as the agents involved imagine their environment as being stable and predictable and act accordingly, their actions will result in maintaining the environment's stability. However, if a competitor adopts different methods, such as a new and more flexible structure, this will augment the turbulence detected by other agents.

This turbulence is therefore not the determining element in our *fin de siècle*. On the other hand, it is the idea of complexity which makes it possible for us to have a better idea of the environment that confronts companies. Complexity and not complication: the essential difference is that complexity is not reducible and we cannot make a model of it. It defies our Cartesian logic. We have known for a long time now that a wave cannot be reduced; it cannot be understood by cutting it into little unitary wavelets. On the other hand, until now we believed that the environments which confronted companies could be reduced and so analyzed; the strategic planning model is a prime example of this. If companies have had to evolve, to reconsider their way of operating, it is because they have been confronted more and more often with phenomena perceived as being complex. We can associate this perceived complexity with two major groups of phenomena: those concerning the intensification of competition linked to the globalization of transactions and to the need to satisfy clients in a different way; and the growing importance of the time factor within competition.

The globalization of the economy is one of the determining factors in the emergence of new competitive pressures. Accessibility is growing in all markets, and interconnections between individuals, more and more difficult to comprehend, have allowed strong competitors to enter the value chain at all levels (Miles and Snow 1992). Moreover, the mass production model is no longer applicable. The nature of production itself has changed; its content is now different. In a context dominated by supply, the important factor is to

1. On this subject see Mintzberg (1993, 1994).
2. The 'Thirty Glorious' years, name given to the continuous growth period following World War II.

control the characteristics of the product, even within a service industry. When competition increases, services play a more and more important role in the creation of value, the product itself losing some of its importance (Quinn 1992). Strategic positioning must be reconsidered; the death knell of generic strategies has tolled, especially that of simple domination by cost or differentiation. Companies can no longer allow themselves to concentrate on macro-segments while neglecting market niches. There is the familiar story of how Western firms have progressively abandoned markets as vast as those of motorcycles and televisions. It is 'mass-customization' that helps firms to stay competitive. Competition therefore leads to paradoxical demands which involve, for example, the continuous delivery of customized and inexpensive products of quality.[3] Organizations must modify their forms and their ways of functioning in order to adapt to these new constraints. Proximity to clients and intimate knowledge of their needs are at the heart of those transformations that interest us here, implying more autonomy in the field and a greater cross-cutting ability.

Another important contingent factor is the control of time. It becomes a crucial element in a company's competitive power. By means of the turbulence that it generates, the increased rate of transactions gives rise to competition based on the ability to adapt and to be increasingly flexible. This more pronounced temporal pressure is based on two elements: the more rapid dissemination of innovation in all domains, and the need to shorten operational cycles (Stalk and Hout 1990). Increased speed in the dissemination of innovations from one sector to another makes it more and more difficult for a company to protect a geographic or industrial territory (Miles and Snow 1992). This faster dissemination of innovation affects all domains, including, of course, technological innovation, but also managerial innovations like re-engineering or the search for total quality. The implications for a firm's internal organization are considerable. A company must attain greater flexibility in order to integrate new elements but must also be capable of reducing the development cycle for new products. An advantage over the development cycle is cumulative, since a few iterations in this cycle should be sufficient to create a dominant product (Gomory and Schmitt 1991). In addition to the domination that is brought about by quicker modifications of a product, a strong competitive advantage can also develop from faster service. Customers attach value to the reduction of delivery time. Companies must therefore be able to play on all of their cycles in order to reduce the elapsed time between order and delivery (Stalk and Hout 1990). The necessary reduction in the cycles of production, delivery, and product development involves an overhaul of a firm's organization towards better

3. See, for example, Pine (1993) and Boynton and Victor (1991).

coordination of the entities that compose it and increased initiative on the part of operating personnel.

When we describe the 'environment' as being a more complex one, we remain at a relatively simple level of analysis, that of an external observer remaining at a global level. An obvious consideration if we further analyze this trend is that this complexity is created for each industry, sector or region by the very same organization that tries to adapt to it. There is no such thing as environment, except as a very convenient and useful reification. Thus our perspective must be that of co-evolution;[4] organizations evolve in response to one another's adaptations. Thus, if new organizational forms and specially the network form as we will describe it in this book become indeed the dominant model, than we are just at the beginning of a competition characterized by its rapidity and complexity.

Transformation towards new organizational forms thus seems inevitable. However, it is carried out in a particularly favorable context; a certain number of facilitating factors serve as catalysts for the evolution in progress. The increased availability of certain resources, in particular human and technological resources, as well as strategies for refocusing groups, were necessary conditions to allow the emergence of network companies. In addition to the faster dissemination of ideas and technologies, the development of new organizational forms rests on two other axes: the improvement in the level of training of individuals and the breakthrough in information technologies. It is therefore in this dual light – the end of a period of great stability and the possibilities offered by the development of generalists who are using new technologies – that one must consider the emergence of new organizational forms.

Employees' ever-increasing level of training allows work organization to be rethought, producing an increase in the autonomy of actors at all levels of the organization. The positions proposed are richer, and they require new capacities for adaptation and above all a better knowledge of the organization, which once more increases the cognitive abilities needed by the individuals involved. Employees at all levels must be increasingly implicated in the organization if evolution towards the reduction of the influence of the center is desired. The peripheral actors must therefore be ready to take on a larger role in decision-making. The evolution of ways of thought – but also the tensions of the job market – permits the company to function more flexibly, with working hours which are continually adapted to the demands of production. The large number of part-time contracts is not excluded from this

---

4. For thorough coverage on co–evolution, see the 1999 special issue of *Organization Science*, **10** (5) Sept-Oct, 1999) and especially the paper by Lewin and Volberda.

trend as more and more companies allow their employees to use their free time to work for other employers.

The improved level of skills of employees also permits optimum use of new technologies. The tools used are of two types. Design tools offer greater flexibility and therefore contribute to the evolution towards the custom-made work and project-by-project work that is often demanded by the customer. The second type of tool is more directly associated with new organizations and concerns communication technologies. These tools can be a decisive aid, in that they lead to opening up the organization both externally and internally. In some cases, they promote the dismantling of the hierarchical system or an improvement in the efficiency of intra-organizational coordination. The organizational phenomena affected by the use of new technologies have an increasingly broader scope since these tools can be used to eliminate the constraints imposed by time and distance. In an optimistic scenario, an interaction between the technological dimension and social dimension can be envisaged: the development of these tools accompanies that of the organization (and vice versa) in the direction of more flexible and less compartmentalized forms.

Refocusing on core competences in response to the increased demands for the central management of groups to create worth and value is indisputably one of the most important elements needed for the appearance of new organizational forms (Foss 2002). Core competence's refocusing is a necessary condition for the emergence of the network company. Indeed, the logic of the network company and that of the conglomerate are quite simply incompatible, for it is the complementary nature of its different businesses that is at the root of the network company's cohesion. Such complementarities do not exist in conglomerate expansion. Core competences thus emerge as the anchoring element in the development of the vision necessary for the cohesion of new organizations. If this refocusing movement is independent and, as is true for numerous companies, if it precedes the modification of their organizations, it will be accompanied by the need for a certain ability to read across. The wave of refocusing, which marked the difficult first years of the 1980s, did in fact continue, establishing this trend as the foundation of an industrial logic of development. This logic, in contrast to the conglomerate approach, is based on the pursuit of cohesion and synergies, which are defined in a broad sense in terms of core competences brought together to satisfy a complex demand that cuts across traditional branches of activity. Refocusing on core competences, in its most recent meaning, can be directly linked to the emergence of new organizational forms: the ability to read across from one unit of the organization to others is needed (Hamel and Prahalad 1989; Markides and Williamson 1994). This refocusing can be linked to the definition of the core competences needed within a company in order to fulfill its mission. The articulation of an organization's core competences and mission thus appear to be both a cause of the new structure and an emerging dimension of that structure. By holding on to this conception of reference to the mission and core competences we acknowledge their existence outside a group of certain individuals who want to exercise a centralizing and cohesive power over the rest of the company. We therefore understand better how the idea of organizational mission can be interpreted within an organization with an emergent center or one which functions without a center. Core competences and mission are therefore a cohesive element for new forms of organization. They have an important role to play within a non-hierarchical structure.

THE TRANSITION TO NETWORKING

The transition to a different organizational approach, which breaks with the hierarchical conception of an organization, becomes apparent in many research trends.[5] The foundations of the network company are numerous and concern several levels of analysis: individuals, organizational sub-units, or entire organizations. The analysis in this work focuses on the level of the organizational sub-unit. At the same time, it must be noted that all these three levels of analysis are inseparable, and therefore we will touch on them in this introduction.

At the individual level, the internal relations within the company, the way in which the role of managers is conceived, and the ways in which the organization can be modeled all evolve under the influence of different converging trends. Thus, we see the appearance of employees who have greater statutory power and who are more autonomous. The role of supervision moves in the direction of becoming one of support.[6] This new role lends itself to the creation of situations that allow each employee to carry out optimal adjustments not only to achieve the goal of greater flexibility, but also to achieve greater pertinence. More room for maneuver is thus given to employees at all levels, controls are relaxed, and work in groups, that often cut across existing structures, is encouraged.

The oldest break with a bureaucratic and controlling approach is found in the trend which places increasing emphasis on human relations, starting from Elton Mayo's founding experiment with workers of the Hawthorne Western Electric plant in Chicago. This trend continues to have consequences at the present time through participatory management, in which the goal is to

5. For instance, Foss (2002) quotes total quality management, business process re-engineering and outsourcing.
6. See, for instance Ezzamel, Lilley and Willmott (1994).

involve a significant number of people in the decision-making process. The same is true for the learning organization which must adopt a way of operating that allows it constantly to call itself into question and to learn from this self-examination. Planning systems, control mechanisms such as goal-oriented management, or incentive programs that are associated with a hierarchical approach all serve to limit the desire of all individuals concerned to learn.[7] These actors restrict themselves to defensive behaviors which inhibit the transition to 'double-loop' learning. It is therefore difficult to envisage learning without real organizational self-examination. Another notion involves the same type of structural adaptation: the notion of entrepreneurship in which an independent champion is at the origin of major innovations in the company.[8] The idea is thus to favor an autonomous process of innovation that functions at the edge of the organization. Controls and planning are reduced in this approach. Risk-taking is emphasized, and the work is done through different project teams. A trend that is particularly active and close to the concerns of those previously mentioned is that of total quality management. This approach is sometimes understood as applying solely to production, but it does of course apply to all aspects of a company. Total quality management requires that a company be reorganized into teams centered around processes which cut across traditional functions, beginning at the level of the producers and finishing at the level of the customers. This reorganization tries to allow each of the teams to contribute to the improvement of the process and to learning (Spencer 1994).

At the global level, there are four ways of imagining the organization of a company that seem to put the new concept of relations within a company in a particularly interesting light: the notion of emergence, organizations analyzed from the angle of chaos, the image of the hologram and the knowledge management perspective. These four means of envisioning a company force us to imagine with a different perspective the role of the center and more generally the role of managers within a company. They thus shed light on our analysis of the evolution towards a network company. A vision emerges of a fluctuating system in which peripheral actors play an important role, and in which the whole is found in each of its parts.

The notion of emergent strategy (Mintzberg and Waters 1985) applies to strategic change. We can distinguish two poles: on the one hand, deliberate strategies based on a detailed and unambiguous initial plan that is understood by all and carried out exactly and, on the other hand, emergent strategies that

---

7. On the links between learning and control mechanisms, one can consult: Mintzberg (1993), Senge (1990), Argyris (1991), and specifically Quinn Mills and Friesen (1992).
8. On intrepreneurship and its organizational implications: Burgelman (1983), Baden-Fuller and Stopford (1993), Block and MacMillan (1993) and Day (1994).

are characterized by a continuity in the unintended processes. Between these two ideal poles there exists a continuum within which all existing strategies can be found. Thanks to these models of the organization, it becomes easier to identify what the hierarchical approach has always forgotten: no matter what the degree of meticulousness used in establishing plans, there is always a component that cannot be managed, that is marked by subjectivity and that is untouched by the rationality attached to the plans and controls (Gabriel 1995). These unmanageable areas seem to expand or at least seem to be better taken into consideration in the agents' own internal models. The network organization better integrates such emergent components and moves clearly towards a project in which the emergent is essential.

Similar lessons can be drawn if the organization is presented as an open, dynamic and non-linear system that is in a chaotic state (Thiétart and Forgues 1995). One of the basic premises of chaos theory is sensitivity to initial conditions. According to this premise, a minute modification of one of the initial parameters can have spectacular effects on the system, and it can therefore go from order to chaos at any given moment. In such a context, it is impossible to plan globally and for the long term. Systems of control and planning therefore seem illusory. In view of this, only an incremental approach is possible, and the central agents must devote themselves to a corresponding role. The idea of self-organization underlies this approach, and we can see how new forms of organization allow companies to respond better to the unpredictability of such a system.

Morgan (1986) presents another image of the company: he suggests seeking out organizational forms that go back to the hologram principle (He also shows that the brain is partly organized in this way, which explains its capacity to integrate a certain complexity.) If the hologram is broken, it can be pieced together again from only one of its elements: in the hologram, the whole is found in each of its parts, and the overall effect results from the combination of the parts. The image of the hologram leads to three main principles for organizations that are flexible and capable of innovation. The first principle is that of redundancy: each of the parts must show a certain polyvalence and reflect the whole. This redundancy must be sufficient to engender greater complexity than that of the environment (principle of necessary variety). The second principle is that of connectivity which ensures the emergence of an order among the different parts; for it is the complexity of the connections which allows complex problems to be resolved. The third principle is one of regulation. Minimal specification is used to prevent the break-up of the organization. Under this model, relations must be clear and methodical so that problems can be solved, but order must be emergent, not imposed. The image of the hologram is particularly rich as a model for the creation of new organizations. In this image are found the principles of self-organization, which call into question the mechanisms of planning and control. It is important to establish degrees of freedom in order to permit adaptation and innovation. These can include specification simply of what is undesirable, while the rest, the goal, remains open for the group of actors.

By focusing on the need to develop and share knowledge, the knowledge management literature is very complementary to the image of the hologram. It offers a global perspective on the firm grounded in the resource-based view. Basically the rationale of this trend is that the ability to manage knowledge represents the foundation of the organizational advantage.[9] This is certainly one of the main drivers for the development of the network organization (Foss 2002). Indeed, an analysis of the knowledge management literature shows the necessity of a radical change in the overall organization. The necessity of autonomy and freedom within the organization is one of the leitmotivs of the knowledge management literature. Ambiguity and even some form of chaos also seem to be among the necessary conditions. There is indeed a contradiction between the vertical orientation of a structure by operation and the need to exchange horizontally the knowledge within the organization.[10] According to Nahapiet and Ghoshal (1998), this results in the necessity for organizations to develop their social capital, that is to say the network links between individuals. One of the archetypal forms of such internal networking is the very popular communities of practice described by Wenger (1999). Communities of practice indeed are very illustrative of the necessity to create spaces of freedom and of exchange within the organization to instill the network logic. In the same vein, Hansen (1999, 2002) insists on the importance of a combination of direct and indirect links between sub-units to enhance knowledge development. This vision of the organization is close to the description made earlier by Nonaka and Takeuchi (1994) of a hypertext organization.

At the level that concerns us directly, that is to say, the relationships between the central unit and the 'peripheral' organizational sub-units, the company follows the example of the external network and gets away from a hierarchical approach, sometimes half-heartedly, but sometimes radically. This movement away from the hierarchical approach is characterized by a series of transformations which can be represented rather well by two principal dimensions: opening-up internally and diminishing the influence of the cente.[11] If companies' networks force themselves to define relationships

---

9. Good examples of such an argumentation can be found in: Kogut and Zander (1992), Winter (1993), Zack (1999), Merali (2000), Nahapiet and Ghoshal (1998).

10. Further developments on the links between structural conditions and knowledge management can be found in Nonaka (1994), Hernes (1999), Ravasi and Verona (2001) and Gupta and Govindarajan (2000).

11. This is also the conclusion proposed by Chakravarthy and Gargiulo (1998).

that defy simple price mechanisms, the network company escapes the burden of hierarchy. In pursuit of that goal, some large companies break up into autonomous sub-units, embark on re-engineering operations, or review their strategic planning. Furthermore, research has presented numerous new global configurations known under a variety of names. Thus a number of trends have arisen from the heterogeneity of the models mentioned.

Since the middle of the 1980s, numerous studies have been published about the transformations of large companies. These large businesses have been evolving away from a bureaucratic mode of functioning towards one that is more organic. Whether the studies deal with descriptions of specific cases, with intervention techniques such as re-engineering, or with the necessary revision of planning methods, the line of attack here is one of change and of improvement of old methods.

There are several studies which have described the transformations of bureaucratic companies. The changes in organization at Lafarge Copée (Feneuille 1990) provide a good example. The company had previously been organized under the matrix model, and it therefore comprised a double hierarchy. The center was then considerably simplified, and the structure was decentralized. The functional structure disappeared, to be replaced by 'flexible interactive networks': as all of the individuals have common concerns, regardless of their occupation, zone or level, they can be made to work together. The company was divided into operational units which all take part in the network activities, and for each project one of these units takes on a leadership position. There are also many large French companies in the public sector that launched restructuring plans leading to dismantling of the hierarchical systems, to decentralization, and to opening-up. EDF-GDF, France Télécom, La Poste (Marmonier and Thiéart 1993), and even the RATP (David 1995) and Renault (Midler 1993) are just some examples of companies in the public sector that underwent such changes. At the heart of these great upheavals are a cross-cutting orientation and a lesser influence of the center, which loses in part its power of command. This change implies an increasing autonomy of sub-units, which in turn accompanies a reduction in the number of hierarchical levels. Project work also fits into this logic.

Re-engineering techniques set out a certain number of elements that are close to the concerns of these transforming bureaucracies. The works of Hammer and Champy (1993) and of the offices of McKinsey have inspired an impressive number of restructurings. The primary concern of re-engineering is the optimization of organizational processes rather than the optimization of each task. A company that has experienced a re-engineering operation shows characteristics that orient it towards an escape from the hierarchical approach: reduction in the number of hierarchical levels, delegation in decision-making, reduction in the number of controls, elimination of standard processes, group work, etc. Re-engineering therefore heads in the direction of a networked company by improving the processes of coordination among different functions. This in turn leads to a cross-cutting organization which calls the hierarchical model strongly into question.

Other important elements in this challenge to the respective roles of center and periphery are the processes of strategic planning and strategy formulation.[12] The former is revised while the latter is experienced differently. The necessity of reworking the concept of strategic planning was due in large part to the poor use of it by the majority of large companies: planning had become a bureaucratic tool that was too rational. Planning therefore had to be rethought in a different light. Thus, planners are being forced to modify their roles in order to become more creative. This change is also affecting the relationship between center and periphery in the process of formulating strategy. It now concerns evolution towards strategies that are emergent. The growing importance of emergent strategies that constantly challenges deliberate choices but also the increased role of each employee in constantly calling into question the choices made are characteristic of the new process of strategy formation.

Resulting from a reorganization process more radical than those described in the previous paragraphs, the network company fits into a rather broad category which corresponds to a wide range of configurations. Descriptions of specific cases, which are quickly established as ideal types, are numerous. They make it difficult to reach a consensus. Nevertheless, certain trends that are close to the concerns already mentioned emerge from these cases. We find two essential elements which account for this evolution towards the networked company: cross-cutting activities linked to a capacity to recombine structures, as well as the smallest possible influence of the center (or the autonomy of the periphery). The cohesion of these new organizations evolves. It changes orientation from a vertical to a horizontal emphasis: the actors autonomously orchestrate the convergence of collective action by making the necessary adjustments. A corollary to this evolution is the dismantling of hierarchy. Because interfaces are assured by mutual adjustments between actors and because the center diminishes as a result, networked companies have organization charts that are horizontal or that have a dramatically reduced number of hierarchical levels. If a more central entity often remains, this entity's size often decreases, while the number of people or coordinated units increases.

Among the first attempts to present an alternative to classic models of organization is the model of the type Z organization by Ouchi and Jaeger

---

12. On the necessity to revisit strategic planning: Lenz and Lyles (1985), Marx (1991), and of course Mintzberg (1993).

(1978), an intermediary configuration between the J-Japanese model and the A-American model. Culture plays a decisive role in this model, but concerns such as consensual decisions and individual responsibility appear already in the type Z model. Another interesting contribution is that of Mintzberg (1980, 1981 and 1989) which presents adhocracy. Adhocracy is above all a type of organization by transversal projects in which there is an absence of control in the classic sense of the term and importance is accorded to the power of ability. The principal themes of the network company are already present in these first configurations, for they show organizations in which the influence of the center diminishes in favor of a larger autonomy of the actors, as well as transversal and ephemeral organizations which are better adapted to diverse projects.

There exist numerous publications which expand on the various exemplary and definitive configurations that have appeared. We present here some of the milestones. One of the most widely accepted versions of these configurations was the N-form (N for new and because it follows M!) put forward by Hedlund (1994). The N form seeks to combine areas of knowledge rather than to divide them up as the multidivisional form did. The N form is characterized by three things: its ability to recombine teams, its lateral networks of communication, and its role as catalyst, architect or protector for management.[13] A related case study done by Quinn Mills and Friesen (1992) deals with the British Petroleum Group, which was completely divided up into independent units and sub-units. In this case study, management activities are carried out by support units, without any line hierarchical connection with operational units. Reduction of the influence of the center is thus pushed to its maximum, while cooperation between units, a necessity to smooth functioning of the group, is simply suggested. Remaining within the same type of approach, Quinn (1992) distinguishes four different forms that are more or less organized into a hierarchy and compartmentalized. Numerous examples of such configurations can also be found in the field of multinational corporation companies.[14] One of the most famous examples is the description of the transnational company described by Bartlett and Ghoshal (1989); this archetype is characterized by a dispersed web of interconnected resources, these resources being located in differentiated sub-units. In such a company,

---

13. See also: the cellular form described by Miles et al. (1997), the case study of Silicon Valley companies by Bahrami (1992), the horizontal organization (Ostoroff 1999; Denton 1991; Graham and LeBaron 1994) or the shamrock organization (Handy 1990).
14. For instance, see Frost (2001) or Gooderham and Ulset (2002).

each business unit takes part to a varying degree in the innovation process, based on their local knowledge; they are specialized and, contrary to what is observed in the classical M-firm, very interdependent.

THE NETWORK PROPOSAL: A PERIPHERAL ISSUE?

Companies are thus evolving towards structures whose central management has a diminishing influence, even in some cases to the point of adopting holographic models – the center is found in each of the peripheral units. As well as this diminution of the central influence, companies are also heading in the direction of opening up between peripheral units. Through different studies of this evolution, a convergent group of trends is emerging, a group of trends to what we can usefully refer to as the network company. Originally, this theme of the network concerned a company's external arrangements, such as relations with subcontractors or partners. These areas have now been studied rather well. On the other hand, the cohesion of organizations composed of autonomous and interdependent units, where plurality is exacerbated, remains largely misunderstood and poorly analyzed. This book, the result of in-depth empirical research, aims to analyze in detail the cohesion of fragmented companies, and to make the assessment of two decades of developments, which calls for a work of consolidation and analysis.

We should note already that the word *network* is used in this book as a metaphor whose limits we must emphasize. First of all, this metaphor serves both to focus the mind of the reader and to present a first definition of our objective. However, if this definition means something, it does not mean the same thing to everybody. The concept of the network company is very broad. It encompasses multiple realities and if we think about it as a typical configuration, it does not permit the rigorous analysis of cohesion within various organizations. It would be possible to establish as an objective the definition of 'ideal-types' of network companies, but as we will see below it seems more pertinent to refer to general principles of organization – the network being one of them – that themselves have a range of ideal-types: the organizational mode.

Thus, for us the network will be above all an organizational mode that can assure the cohesion of the organization or that can at least strongly contribute to the cohesion of that organization. The network (Jarillo 1988) finds its place alongside the three organizational modes proposed by Ouchi (1979, 1980): the market, the bureaucracy, and the clan. We are interested in the emergence of firms in which autonomous relationships between units (which are autonomous themselves) decisively contribute to the cohesion of the group. This trend can be analyzed as the result of a growing importance given to the network as a mode of organization.

A salient element of these issues is the role played by the periphery in the cohesion of a company. The center steps aside in order to put into place the autonomous links between peripheral units that are at the heart of this cohesion. The focus of the network organization is therefore on the peripheral operational units, which, through the transversal relationships they maintain, now play a central role in the cohesion of the organization. To give priority to the study of the peripheral units, and not simply and exclusively to examination of the center, is an essential element of this research project. It is indeed at this level that flexibility, as well as the capacity to innovate and look after clients, emerges. If the center no longer imposes itself on the entire organization, the periphery makes the decisions, and in this case cohesion can result from the interactions among these peripheral units.

Therefore, the first step in an approach that aims to clarify our understanding of the functioning of networks must be to improve our knowledge of the notion of organizational modes and, in particular, the role played by the network in the cohesion of an organization. This is admittedly the object of the entire book, but the first foundations will be laid by defining a general conceptual framework. These concepts will then be developed by empirical investigations. In very concrete terms, we will highlight the mechanisms by which the network can constitute an internal organizational mode that contributes to organizational cohesion.

As an organizational mode, the network is based on the relationships between peripheral units. It is therefore essential that the impact of these relationships be evaluated and that we see how far this autonomous functioning can go without the intervention of the center. We will therefore study the nature of the links between peripheral units in a detailed and systematic manner in four company cases. However, if the network takes on greater importance within a company, the other organizational modes do not necessarily disappear. It is therefore necessary to evaluate in what ways complementarities or incompatibilities can appear among these different organizational modes and understand how the network combines with the other forms of organization, in particular, the market, the bureaucracy, and the clan. Another essential question, which is complementary to the preceding one and which also merits a response, is that of the role of the center and of the very necessity of its existence. Tasks that cannot be carried out by the periphery and that necessitate the intervention of a central unit, whether it be emergent or not, must be called into question.

THE RESEARCH METHOD

The questions raised in the preceding paragraph call for fundamental empirical work. This book focuses on three years of research done in four French companies: Air Liquide (air gases), CFDP (an insurance company), Colas (road resurfacing) and GTIE (electric installations). These companies were selected because of the importance they have attached to a decentralized and cross-cutting approach to their management. Two of these companies are the world leaders in their activities (Air Liquide and Colas); the other two rank among the national leaders. The companies have also established a direct link between their organization and their performance.

Air Liquide is the world's foremost producer and distributor of air gases (oxygen, hydrogen, carbon dioxide, rare gases, etc.). The group is strongly internationalized, with its European market share representing only 55% of its turnover. Air Liquide has completely reworked its organization around small, very self-sufficient units, with horizontal structures that are interconnected. There are essentially three types of peripheral structures: service groups for each country, national production establishments and customer service centers that handle production, sales and distribution on a local basis. The research carried out for this study has looked in detail at a national establishment and at one region (or customer service center).

CFDP is an insurance company dealing in legal protection. It is among the top three French companies in this sector. Its products are for the most part intended for individuals to whom, for a fee, CFDP provides legal assistance in the case of litigation and financing of lawyers in the case of lawsuits. Their direct clients are insurance intermediaries (brokers or agents) that insure the distribution of insurance policy contracts to individuals. The company is composed of about one hundred employees (or 'delegates')[15] for all of France. There were two elements that appeared particularly worth noting in the operation of CFDP. First, the company adheres to a strategy that aims at developing relationships with its insurance intermediary clientele which go beyond simple commercial contacts. In order to favor collective reflection on the company's future and that of the insurance intermediary's profession, all decision-making is done through the collaboration, in equal numbers, of CFDP delegates (made up of the company's salaried employees) and the insurance intermediaries (the company's clients). The second interesting element lies in the organization of the company. The two major shareholders want to promote new relationships within the company, both being persuaded that the secondary objective of economic profitability will follow. They have

---

15. A delegate is responsible for the conception and diffusion of an insurance contract for a specific district.

thus been trying to associate the delegates with strategic decision-making, through varied systems of representation. CFDP can be considered as an experiment and, at the same time, as a model of what can be done in a larger organization.

Colas is the world leader in road construction. Its organization is distinctive in respect of the considerable autonomy left to its basic peripheral units: the agencies. This strong self-sufficiency, which is relatively uncommon in the sector, is one of the key elements in the group's competitiveness. It is therefore very interesting to note here that this necessary autonomy is accompanied by a strong need for integration. Taking this into consideration, the Colas case is particularly rich in lessons.

GTIE, a subsidiary of the Vivendi group, is involved in the construction and electrical engineering sectors. Its organizational mode is particularly interesting and is based on the principle of seeking 'interlinking' between its autonomous units. This operation is intended to enable direct growth in the profitability of the entire group. The group is composed of 700 'companies' with or without the status of subsidiary, each comprising between approximately 20 and 120 people. Each company is distinguished by the specific nature of its own strategic project. Each time a new project is identified within a company, an internal spin-off takes place, and a new structure is created. Therefore there are numerous complementarities within the group, as much horizontal as vertical. Units are encouraged to meet, and some formal networks do exist.

The framework of this research is that of multiple embedded cases. This approach consists in analyzing, within each case study, several sub-units that are considered as mini-cases. Hence, we make our analyses of the organization of each company in the study in two parts. The first part consists of in-depth interviews that allow us to construct for ourselves an initial model of the structure at an aggregate level. The second part begins in each of the cases with the selection of sub-units that become the object of a study in more depth. This study takes place by using sociometric questionnaires, that is to say, questionnaires about the relationships between individuals in these units. In this way, it is possible to obtain a much more refined model of the structures, an inter-individual representation. The data is then consolidated case by case and thereafter across all four cases.

This book will not retrace the whole process of data consolidation for each case. The general elements can be found in the annexes. The objective of this book is to present the reader with the conclusions of the research and the results concerning the network organization.

STRUCTURE OF THE BOOK

This book contains six chapters, in addition to this general introduction, which setout the conceptual framework of the research and then analyze and discuss its results. Chapter 2 explains in detail the conceptual framework of the research. It is based on the concept of organizational modes. The chapter demonstrates how the analysis (in terms of these organizational modes) can bring about progress through the cumulation of knowledge. Direct reference is made to organizational configurations and to a certain conception of the institutional approach in order to dismiss them. This chapter contains all the elements necessary for the reader who seeks to understand the author's conceptual approach.

Chapters 3 to 7 present the empirical results of the research. Chapter 3 studies the reasons for becoming an internally networked organization. Beyond the theoretical statements already made in the first part of this work, this chapter evaluates what the actors have retained from the approach and what they highlight when they are forced to assess the results.

Chapters 4 and 5 discuss exclusively the relationships between peripheral units. They describe concretely how cross-cutting operations, without any intervention from the center, can assure the cohesion of the organization. These mechanisms of network cohesion are illustrated with numerous examples taken from the cases studied, with additional attention being paid to the difficulties of implementation. Chapter 4 deals with transfers and cross-cutting projects between the peripheral units. Chapter 5 focuses on collaborative work which has less material significance: the transfer of skills and the collective formulation of strategy. It then goes on to describe the organization as a community of peripheral units by studying the mechanisms of an emerging convergence among the units.

Chapter 6 deals more particularly with the role of the center and the connection between the network organization and its center. It seems indeed that certain roles, especially those of representation, must be filled by a central agency, possibly an emergent one.

Chapter 7 examines organizational cohesion as a result of the combination between the four modes of organization. The links between the network and the other modes of organization are examined in detail.

In the conclusion, we present the difficulties associated with transition towards the network in a cross-cutting way and we emphasize the levers of action available to the decision-maker. We finally propose an approach to implementation broken up into a series of key steps.

2. The network, a mode of organization

New organizational forms, networked firms, company networks, remodeled companies: these are all characterized by their heterogeneity, by the particular way in which each one of them organizes its economic and social relationships and by how they attain a certain level of cohesion. This singularity makes it difficult to categorize any particular entity. The notion of configuration for representing a category of organizations is undoubtedly useful but of limited scope, to the extent that one might expect a complex and unpredictable mixture of ideal types.

Analysis and understanding of an institution or of a particular type of institution, its coherence, and the way its economic and social relationships are organized can only be made in relation to general principles of organization, themselves being of an 'ideal-typical' nature. The idea of the means of control developed by Ouchi (1979, 1980) and later elaborated upon by Jarillo (1988) for proposing modes of organization meets this demand. Modes of organization make it possible to give an account of organizational cohesion for any particular institution however specific this institution is. Moreover, they have the added advantage of allowing for more complete understanding of the emergence of the network organization whose cohesion depends essentially on the network as a mode of organization. The analyses of the four cases and their results as presented in the following chapters are based on an understanding of the organization as structured around four modes of organization: the market, bureaucracy, the clan, and the network. This conceptual framework has served as a guide for the collection and processing of data and will be presented in the first part of this chapter.

Taking the notion of the mode of organization into account thus encourages us to reconsider the question of the network company. Network organizations become organizations in which the network, as an organizational mode, plays a particular role. It is the role of the network in the cohesion of organizations that this book aims to analyze. The second part of this chapter compares the author's adopted conceptual framework with two other approaches frequently used for analyzing network companies: the configurational approach and certain aspects of the institutional approach. The object of this theoretical discussion is to show the need for taking into account the concept of mode of organization if one really wants to advance in understanding the actual operations of network companies.

ANALYSIS BY MODES OF ORGANIZATION

Analysis, in terms of modes of organization and particularly in terms of the network's contribution to the organization, allows for a formalization of our thoughts about the network company. It is in fact this networked mode of organization, in contributing strongly (but not exclusively) to the cohesion of new organizational forms, that gives rise to its originality. Recent developments can thus be interpreted as giving greater importance to networking as a mode of organization in the cohesion of the organization. Using the notion of mode of organization, it becomes possible to analyze this recent development of numerous organizations, each of which has its own specificity, in a comparative manner. In this work, we have gone beyond the single case in order to understand the elements characteristic of the development of companies in all sectors for some fifteen years now.

General Conceptual Framework

The concept of the mode of organization is derived directly from that of the *mode of control* (Ouchi 1979, 1980). These modes of control are mechanisms that make it possible to assure the mediation of transactions in any institution. The concept concerns major principles of organization (the term 'control' is inappropriate when it comes to the market and the network) that help assure cohesion within the companies involved. It is important not to confuse any one institution, such as a network of companies for example, with the network as a mode of organization. The term 'network' can mean both an organizational logic (i.e. a mode of organization) and a particular group of companies that cooperate. In the conceptual framework used in this research, the network, bureaucracy, the market and the clan are considered as organizational logics that could be found in any particular institution. We shall see that each company uses each of these modes of organization to a greater or lesser extent.

The first thoughts about the modes of organization did not consider the network as a distinct logic in and of itself. They were only interested in the market and bureaucracy[16] (Imai and Itami 1984) or in the market, bureaucracy

---

16. See also the more recent discussion by Foss (2002) and the work by Zenger (2002).

and the clan (Ouchi 1979, 1980). The network as a mode of organization started late as a topic for theoretical reflection, but the notion did begin to emerge little by little as the organization of companies evolved towards more cross-cutting horizontal links and less hierarchy. This new mode appeared in several publications in the late 1980s and in the 1990s, either directly under the name of 'network' or under the name of 'trust'.[17] One of the most remarkable and early efforts to synthesize the subject was made by Jarillo (1988) who, inspired by the works of Ouchi (1979, 1980), proposed a model of the four modes of organization in two dimensions: the dimension of 'approach to the relation' on one hand, and that of the 'legal form' on the other.

The synthesis of this research leads us to define four modes of organization with ideal-typical properties whose combination allows us to review the way cohesion can be obtained in any institution. The modes concern the market, bureaucracy, the clan, and the network (see Figure 2.1). These four modes of organization are distinguished in one dimension by their use of cooperative or non-cooperative relationships and in the other by whether they have a hierarchical or non-hierarchical way of operating.

	Non-cooperative	Cooperative
Non-hierarchical mode of organization	**MARKET**	**NETWORK**
Hierarchical mode of organization	**BUREAUCRACY**	**CLAN**

Figure 2.1 The four modes of organization

Source: adapted from Jarillo 1988

The approach to the relation

The dimension of the 'approach to the relation' defines the spirit in which the organizational actors' activity will take place. This dimension fits perfectly

---

17. Even if network is often used (Eccles and Crane 1987, Jarillo 1988, Powell 1990), trust was used for instance by Bradach and Eccles (1989) in order to name the same organizational mode.

with analysis in terms of the mode of organization: whatever the particular institution we observe, its actors are organized in a logical way that is more or less favorable for carrying out transactions in a satisfactory manner.

To clarify what is meant by the approach to the relation, we might look at game theory[18] and distinguish cooperative games from non-cooperative ones. This way, one can get an elementary idea of the distinction between, on the one hand, the market and the bureaucracy, which are both characterized by a non-cooperative game, and, on the other hand, the network and the clan, which are both characterized by a cooperative game. In the first case, the agents involved will take a short-term perspective and will pursue their own short-term interests before the common interest. In the second case, the common interest is prioritized and a long-term perspective is taken (the agents perceive that it is in their interest to play cooperatively).

The transaction cost theory can serve here to structure thought and to help us better to understand cooperative and non-cooperative relationships. It is worthwhile as well to take account of some points that have recently been suggested by some of the theory's skeptics. The behavioral hypothesis that underlies the transaction cost theory is that of opportunism, which is defined as a pursuit of personal interest that entails the notion of deceit (Williamson 1985). Two of the modes of organization fit Williamson's perspective because they are based on the need for protecting the organization *ex ante* against the possibility of opportunistic behavior on the part of the actors. Obviously, the two modes concerned are the market and bureaucracy. From this perspective, it is important to implement systems of incentives (in the case of the market) and mechanisms of hierarchical control (in the case of bureaucracy). These coercive mechanisms have a direct effect on opportunistic behavior, yet at the same time have a perverse effect. They reinforce the propensity for behaving in an opportunistic manner as soon as one gets a chance to do so. By favoring a non-cooperative approach, they encourage the individual to exploit the weaknesses of the system of control. It is equally important to take into account mechanisms based on a more positive conception of human nature, but this is an approach that Williamson does not seem ready to integrate into his version of the transaction cost theory.[19]

18. Jarillo (1988) used game theories; he distinguished between zero sum games and non-zero sum games. It is necessary to underline that game theorists argue that if there is an exchange, both parties find an interest in the exchange and this interest is perceived, hence the game is not a zero-sum one. The negotiation process might be a zero-game sum in the market transaction, but we are trying here to analyze the transaction itself. Thus, in the market, as well as in the bureaucracy, the game is a non-zero sum game.
19. For a more detailed discussion of this issue, see the debate between Ghoshal and Moran (1996) and Williamson (1996) in the *Academy of Management Review*.

The alternative is thus a cooperative approach to relationships where the modes of organization are based on the hypothesis that individuals have the desire to cooperate. Under certain conditions, it is possible to accept the absence of opportunistic behavior on the part of the agents as a basic hypothesis. Organization by clan or by network corresponds to this case: trust between the parties and the existence of common values allow one to consider the risk of opportunism as negligible. In these two cases, the transaction costs associated with the need to protect oneself against opportunism can be reduced. The costs of negotiation, the costs of writing contracts and the costs of control are lower. It is no longer necessary to implement complicated systems of reciprocal incentives, and the selection of partners is facilitated (Chiles and McMackin 1996). Even if we consider that a residual risk of opportunism exists, its cost can be considered negligible, and the costs necessary for protecting against this residual opportunism are prohibitive. Exchanges thus follow a logic of cooperation that goes beyond the mere short term and is based on trust (in the case of the network) or on common values (in the case of the clan).

The existence of hierarchical bonds

The second dimension that helps structure our conceptual framework resides in the existence or non-existence of hierarchical bonds.[20] By hierarchical bond, we mean the possibility of giving orders, of indicating or modifying the behavior of individual actors or collective subordinates. The fact that hierarchical bonds exist does not imply that they are limited to a single firm: these ties can exist between two firms, for example, between that which places orders and a subcontractor. The existence of hierarchical bonds only implies that a legitimate, but not necessarily statutory, authority has the means of exerting real control. On another note, the fact that hierarchical bonds exist in a particular institution implies that its cohesion can partly be explained by the clan or by bureaucracy. However, in the same institution, certain transactions can essentially be a matter of organization by the network, which means adopting a logic that is non-hierarchical or only

---

20. The second dimension proposed by Jarillo (1988) is that of the legal form which allows him to differentiate the integrated hierarchy (i.e. the firm), organized by the bureaucracy and the clan on the one hand, from the external relations on the other hand, organized by the market and the network. We can only underline the intrinsic contradiction between the use of the concept of mode of organization and the distinction made between these organizational modes depending on the legal form. This would lead us to consider the existence of two modes of organization existing in two legal forms. If we come back to the analysis of Ouchi (1979, 1980), the differentiation between the clan and the bureaucracy on the one hand and the market on the other hand derives from the existence of a legitimate authority, which confirms our choice.

hierarchical in part. Thus we have a second division, between the market and the network, both non-hierarchical modes of organization, on the one hand, and bureaucracy and the clan, which are both hierarchical modes of organization, on the other hand. As defined, this second dimension complies with the logic of modes of organization because it cuts across different institutions.

The Four Modes of Organization

It is now necessary to specify how the cohesion of the company relates to the modes of organization as they have been defined above. The logics of the market, the bureaucracy and the clan are already well outlined in the literature and will be introduced only briefly. By contrast, the network will be the subject of a more detailed analysis. The mechanisms used by a firm to activate each mode of organization will be set out. It is appropriate thereafter to delve into the conditions necessary for the mobilization of a mode of organization. These necessary conditions are the prerequisites; they involve the information or the norms that serve as foundations for the mode of organization.

The informational prerequisites are specific to each of the modes of organization: the market relies on a system of prices, bureaucracy on a set of rules, the clan on traditions, and the network on knowledge of the complementarity of resources among its members.

Depending on the mode of organization concerned, the normative prerequisites can include the existence of common values and beliefs, a legitimate authority, and in every case a rule of reciprocity that ensures the equity of transactions. The prerequisites refer to the basic social consensus that all parties must share in order for a transaction to be organized according to a particular mode. Table 2.1 summarizes the prerequisites[21] necessary for implementing each particular mode of organization. Though this table shows the minimal conditions necessary to put a particular mode of organization into operation, it does not mean that the other elements are not present in the organization studied. Thus, if we take the example of the market mode of organization, transactions are assured as long as the system of prices functions. The use of a pure market mechanism to balance transactions does not require the convergence of values or the intervention of a legitimate authority figure. It is clear that there are markets as institutions that are regulated by a legitimate authority (the State or a professional body) and

---

21. For a more detailed account of the prerequisites for the bureaucracy, the clan, and the market, see Ouchi (1979, 1980).

whose actors share a certain number of values. However, it is not the institution, but rather the mode of organization that interests us.

In the following sections, each mode of organization is presented by giving more detail of the normative and informational prerequisites. We then go on to show how the company can mobilize the mode of organization studied. Emphasis is placed particularly on the network and on the evolution towards a diminished role for bureaucratic mechanisms.

Table 2.1 Normative and informational prerequisites

MODE OF ORGANIZATION	NORMATIVE PREREQUISITES	INFORMATIONAL PREREQUISITES
Market	• Effect of reputation	• System of prices
Bureaucracy	• Legitimate authority	• Rules
Clan	• Legitimate authority	• Traditions
	• Common norms and values	
Network	• Effect of reputation	• Complementarities of resources
	• Common norms and values	

The market

The market is characterized by a non-hierarchical form and by the existence of a non-cooperative game. The market operates thanks to a system of prices. For a market without friction, price contains all of the information necessary for the equity of a transaction. Only one thing is unknown: the honesty of the parties involved. Admittedly, one norm of reciprocity ensures that 'should one party in a market transaction attempt to cheat another, that the cheater, if discovered, will be punished by all members of the social system, not only by the victim and his or her partners' (Ouchi 1979, p. 838). Thus a social consensus must exist which implies that any individual who has devoted himself to cheating must be eliminated from the market by all the other actors. Not all economists agree with this hypothesis which acknowledges the existence of the effect of reputation. It implies that the market has a form of memory that allows everyone to know those actors who have not kept their word and who are not trustworthy. The hypothesis nonetheless appears justified in an organizational analysis whose goal is to get as close as possible to a realistic description, rather than to a theoretical model.

The market can be introduced within the firm by means of two principal mechanisms: systems of internal transfers and remuneration based on performance. Internal transfer prices require that a firm be divided up into profit centers. The divisions may be larger or smaller, ranging from a large sub-unit to a single individual. The principle is then to fix internal transfer prices for the merchandise or for services exchanged between the different centers. For example, an IT department could bill internally for its services in the same way that it could bill an external client company. The logic of these profit centers can be pushed quite far; some companies operate by billing for services rendered from general management to the subsidiaries.

However, it is difficult to reproduce market mechanisms internally. It is rare that a company's internal market possesses the characteristics necessary for operating in a way that is uniquely founded on a price system. The internal market causes too much friction. To operate properly, internal transfer prices must generally be confronted with an external market. One of the radical but efficient means of organizing this confrontation is the opening of the internal market onto the company's exterior one. The internal entities can be placed in competition with external service providers. Thus regulation of internal transactions and the maintenance of competitiveness are obtained through this confrontation with the external market. In some cases, several internal units can even be found in competition with one another; the market then plays an even stronger regulatory role.

In order for the internal system of prices to have a real regulatory impact, there must be a strong link between the contribution of an internal entity or individual and their remuneration. This is the principle of management by objectives when it is associated with variable compensation or with piecework. Management by objectives joined with variable remuneration can be thought of as the annual price negotiation that the employer will have to pay if the objectives are to be reached. If a price system involving few tensions is really established within a company, each unit and/or employee can be compensated according to their real contribution (Ouchi 1979).

It is important to note that a price system within the firm is not synonymous with output control or with control by results. As we shall see later, control by output does not necessarily imply that pay is made according to performance. It can in fact be used in the context of a bureaucratic procedure. Furthermore, profit centers, as they are often conceived in organizations, are more a matter for bureaucratic mechanisms than for market mechanisms. In fact, they often serve as aids to the evaluation of the performance of individuals or units by the superior rank in the hierarchy. An even stronger bureaucratization can arise if problems in internal transactions appear that require hierarchical intervention (Ouchi 1979). In such circumstances, the price system does not reach its real goal of leading to true internalization of the organizational aims by the actors themselves.

Admittedly, one should be relatively prudent in evaluating the contributions of market mechanisms to the internal operations of a particular company. However, the cases studied will give us the opportunity to show the way in which market mechanisms can be put to work effectively and will illustrate in particular the ambiguity of their interactions with network mode of organization.

The Bureaucracy

Bureaucracy corresponds to a non-cooperative game regulated by hierarchical bonds. Bureaucratic control implies the recognition of a legitimate authority that allows the performance of the individuals or entities subjected to bureaucratic organization to be influenced (control by input) or audited (control by output). Here, authority is of the rational-legal type. The role of the hierarchical center is twofold. First of all, it consists in designing a system of rules that must be communicated to subordinate entities or individuals and applied by them. This system of rules constitutes the informational prerequisite necessary to organization by bureaucracy. The center must also ensure the reciprocity of the transaction by: ' • placin g a value on each contribution and then compensating it fairly. The perception of equity in this case depends upon a social agreement that the bureaucratic hierarchy has the legitimate authority to provide this mediation.' (Ouchi 1980, p. 130).

In the internal organization framework, one finds organization by bureaucracy at different levels of analysis. An employee exchanges a salary for his or her submission to the hierarchical superior who directs or evaluates his or her activities. As for the functional or operational sub-units, resources are allocated to these units, and the influence of control or planning is exercised over the use of these resources. At both levels of structure, one can thus distinguish control by input and control by output.

Control by input corresponds to the involvement of the center in the decisions made by the individuals of peripheral units. Thus, the center directly influences the behavior of the actors within the peripheral units beyond any consideration of the ensuing results of these behaviors. In this respect, one of the essential levers of action exerted over peripheral units is intervention in strategy formulation. Strategy review, whether it is completed or not by informal contact in both directions, is an important tool for ensuring the coherence of the strategic project. The allocation of resources that is often associated with strategy review is important as well. The center can also develop strategic themes that define what the company's overall distinctive competences will become. For each operational unit, the center can set grand strategic objectives or make specific suggestions.

Control by output corresponds to *ex post* evaluation of the peripheral units' performance. The center of large companies cannot in fact exert a planning influence on all of the activities or individuals of the peripheral units. Thus delegation to actors from the periphery becomes necessary. This approach was developed throughout the 1950s and is still in use today in many companies. This philosophy of management was pushed to the extreme by Harold Geneen (1984) when he instituted a veritable cult of numbers at ITT. At that time in ITT no explanation was allowed to justify an objective that was not reached. Thus, in the logic of decentralization, the center's influence is not necessarily effaced. On the contrary, influence can assert itself in a much harsher way via control of results. This type of control allows the center to ensure the cohesion of the entire organization around a financial logic.

An important number of studies that subscribe to the hierarchical approach have sought to find a fit between environmental factors and the design of tools of control. The concern of these different studies has been the following: what can be done so that the center best ensures the cohesion of the organization by exerting its influence in a manner adapted to the circumstances? Studies of control indicate what balances can be conceived between controls by input and by output. The analysis of these equilibria is generally made without envisaging the possibility of a reduction of the influence exerted by the center. This influence must be exerted either *ex ante* or *ex post* in order to avoid the loss of cohesion and the break-up of the organization. The search for a 'fit' between strategy, the environment and the method of management of the periphery is the basis of a great number of studies. This contingent trend effectively illustrates the domination of the hierarchical paradigm in the minds of some researchers up until the beginning of the 1990s.

To reach a synthesis, it can be said that the adjustment of the control tool lies in the fork of a dilemma between the two approaches of control by input or by output. The organization must decide between adjusting behavior by determining the periphery's strategy (which limits its possibilities of adaptation) and controlling by performance indicators, which does not allow the center to be involved in prioritizing objectives. The dilemma comes from the fact that it is difficult to hold an operational unit responsible for the results ensuing from behavior (i.e. strategies) that it has not chosen itself. Therefore, arbitration between control by input and control by output must take place.

Goold and Campbell's synthesis (1987) of center/periphery relations corresponds exactly to the fix on the image that we wish to present before analyzing the question of cohesion in relation to the appearance of new organizational forms. In their research, the authors emphasize eight styles of management (see Figure 2.2). Three of these are dominant − strategic planning, strategic control, and financial control − because they correspond to a balance between the influence of control (i.e. control by output) and the influence of planning (i.e. control by input). The role played by bureaucracy in organizational cohesion is considered to be adapted to these three styles. The center's influence is not too pronounced and paralysing for the organization, nor is it too weak which, say the authors, would run the risk of calling the cohesion into question. The other styles are unbalanced because in the absence of cohesion resulting from the center's influence (or if this influence is too strong), the company is no longer competitive.

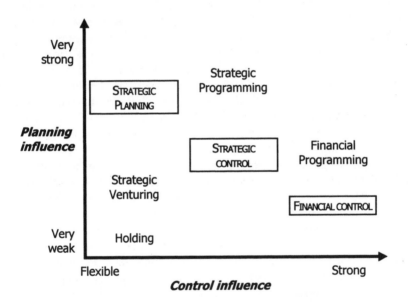

Figure 2.2 The management styles

Source: Goold and Campbell 1987

By means of bureaucratic mechanisms, the influence of the center can ensure the cohesion of the organization. The center regulates and allows for the balance of the structure by taking care of the planning and the control of the activity of the periphery. The periphery appears as a group of operational units under the control of the center and submits to the heavier or lighter discretionary influence of the center. From this point on, the question of cohesion is no longer a concern as it has been resolved by the exertion of central power that regulates all activities of the company. The recent evolution of companies can be interpreted as resulting from a reduction in the controls by input and output exerted by the center. Cohesion is based decreasingly on bureaucratic mechanisms, and a reduction in the influence exerted on one of the dimensions of control no longer necessarily means a reinforcement of the other dimension.

The clan

The clan is characterized by a cooperative game and a hierarchical structure. This mode of organization uses culture and is based on socialization: individuals, once appropriately socialized, will tend to adopt behaviors in accordance with the general objectives of the center. The legitimate authority here takes on a traditional form and is founded on the sharing of common values and beliefs as to what appropriate behavior is. It is the guarantor of the system of norms and values and decides whether behavior is acceptable or not in regard to this system. Socialization allows individuals to internalize the set of rules, the majority of which are informal, that Ouchi (1980) calls traditions. The knowledge of traditions contains all the information necessary for transactions. The reciprocity of the transaction is ensured by the center in relation to the system of norms and values. Performance is not necessarily included among the elements taken into account.

Management has certain methods that allow it to encourage the convergence of beliefs within the firm. Recruitment is a first lever and is notably carried out on the basis of criteria of pre-socialization or 'sociability,' rather than on those of competence. Socialization is then encouraged through the policy of career development. The latter may include an initial course that is more or less long and constraining and can emphasize internal mobility. Furthermore, training efforts can be geared towards socialization. An organizational vision constructed around the company's key competences can also help individuals to adjust their actions.

The clan can become a very efficient mode of organization. It seems particularly pertinent when all measures become difficult (Ouchi 1979). However, the clan remains very exposed to opportunistic behavior if such behavior is not eliminated by the existence of common values (Ouchi 1980).

The network

The network mode of organization is non-hierarchical, and the approach to the relation can be represented by a cooperative game. Normative prerequisites for operating in a network are of two kinds: the rule of reciprocity and the existence of norms and of common values. Indeed, the large majority of studies of the network mode stress two central ideas that are essential to its specificity: the necessity of trust between its actors that fits the notion of norms and common values, as well as the existence of an interdependence between its members or, at the very least, an exchange of resources. The knowledge of resources and skills that the network's members have constitutes the informational prerequisite necessary for transactions to take place. Complementarities, associated with the effect of reputation, make exclusion from the network detrimental for any member having shown himself untrustworthy. After having spelt out the normative and informational prerequisites for the networked organization, we shall discuss some aspects of the possibility of non-hierarchical operations.

The network is based first of all on a relationship of trust. However, this first normative prerequisite needs to be explained. One of the definitions proposed by Chiles and McMackin shows the ties it keeps with opportunism; they argue that trust: 'may be defined as the expectation that an exchange partner will not engage in opportunistic behavior, even in the face of countervailing short-term incentives and uncertainty about long-term benefits' (Chiles and McMackin, 1996 p. 85). Thus, even in an instance where opportunism is sure to be profitable in the short term or where it is not certain that long term gain is conceivable, trusting partners will not engage in opportunism.

Aside from the existence of common social norms, two interpretations of the construction of bonds of trust can be found (Chiles and McMackin 1996). The first interpretation is that of game theory. Cooperation thus appears to be the result of the reflection of agents who are confronted with the multiple game version of the prisoner's dilemma. In the static one-off version of the game, it is non-cooperation that is adhered to. By contrast, the anticipation of future transactions with the same partners stifles opportunistic behavior. As a result, people play a game which becomes cooperative. Granovetter (1985) adds an interesting perspective – that of social interaction. Individuals are indeed involved in social networks which discourage opportunism and have a tendency to favor trust. It is thus a shared past and the existence of social ties that inhibit opportunistic behavior and allow trust to become established. The decision to cooperate therefore results in both a rational calculation of anticipated gain in the framework of a game with multiple plays and a feeling of confidence towards individuals with whom social ties are strong. Furthermore, there is a virtuous circle between the attitude of trust and behavior which embodies trust: a feeling of trust will tend to evoke a positive behavior (for example, the transmission of information), which itself will improve the feeling of trust (Chiles and McMackin 1996). Therefore, one finds the same type of positive feedback as that which brings about a reinforcement of the inclination towards opportunism by means of mechanisms of control.

The rule of reciprocity of the network dictates the exclusion of individuals who are not worthy of trust. This rule of reciprocity is based partly on the effect of reputation, which ensures its application, and also on complementarities between its members that can lead to an interdependence which would make any exclusion costly. However, the network remains a fragile organizational mode since there is no systematic control of the solid foundation of the trust. Thus it is probable that opportunistic behavior exists and will possibly even continue. It still holds true that the effects of reputation diminish opportunism and that behavior linked with trust reinforces this trust. When trust is established, the cost of residual opportunism is less than the costs of the transactions that controlling such opportunism would need.

The effects of reputation can play an essential role in maintaining trust and thus in maintaining the network. Transactions between members of an institution cannot happen according to the network mode unless all the members participating in the transaction share the feeling of trust, which would mean that each one benefits from the reputation of being trustworthy. This reputation is founded on a record of having renounced opportunistic behavior. If an actor no longer has this reputation, no other actor will want to engage in a transaction with him without having costly safeguards. It is therefore probable that this untrustworthy actor will no longer find any partners among those members with good reputations.

Exclusion from the network takes on another form in the particular framework of a company (internal relationships). In this case, one can anticipate a return to bureaucratic organization. So a unit that does not respect the rules of the game will see its autonomy called into question; the center can again intervene and, in certain cases, discipline actors from the periphery. One must keep in mind that the power of the center is largely discretionary. The center can decide to steer the organization towards the network mode by reducing its influence, but it can also go back on this, especially in cases where a peripheral unit does not respect the rules of the game.

Aside from the reduced transaction costs that are made possible by the network organization, transactions depend upon complementarities among its members that can lead to interdependence. The existence of interdependence makes exclusion from the network particularly costly. This interdependence is based on a sharing of resources that can take two forms, those of a specialized unit and of a non-specialized one.

In the first form, a member has access to resources held by other members and devotes himself to creating value in his specific domains. The members of the network are therefore complementary and highly specialized. Each member develops his or her distinctive skills in a particular competitive field. The members thus use their resources in smaller fields where they can be of higher value. Furthermore, the team of members covers a much greater competitive field, as each one is able to mobilize resources held by the other members. Two forms of complementarity can therefore exist: horizontal complementarity and vertical complementarity. Horizontal complementarity can take the shape of specialization by business or by geographic zone. In specialization by business, each member of the network masters a skill that allows for the use or realization of common projects. In specialization by geographic zone, the members cover a greater territory. They can thus propose an overall service that relies on the entire set of local team members. Moreover, they can develop together competences or pool locally available resources. Vertical complementarity relates to the type of specialization that we will call 'upstream downstream'; suppliers and clients (internal or external) contribute their specific knowledge to carrying out a common project. In vertical specialization there is the possibility of developing resources in a precise field, while at the same time being able to benefit from access to the resources of the other units.

The second way to pool resources concerns members who are not differentiated one from the other: there is thus no specialization within the network. The members all have the same role. However, pooling these resources assures access to some resources outside the network. Such cases can be found within a company where distinct units distribute competing products in order to increase the overall market share of the group. Units can then certainly pool their resources.

The link between interdependence and confidence is really a recursive relationship. The sharing of resources, the complementarity of roles, and collaborative work are transformed into interdependence in the context of a climate of trust. The actors accept this mutual dependence because of the sense of confidence that they feel towards one another, and they therefore accept being exposed to the opportunism of other actors. This interdependence in turn reinforces the trust between linked individuals (Johanson and Mattson 1992). This recursivity effectively demonstrates the importance of the role played by the hostages model (Williamson 1985) or other incentive structures in the maintenance of the network; these mechanisms, thanks to their continuous link with trust, can be very efficient, even if one of the parties finds itself less involved than the other. They are not however at the heart of the cohesion acquired via the network; this cohesion is above all based on trust and the sharing of complementary resources.

One of the fundamental elements of the network company is the interdependence between the units that make it up. It is in fact the necessity to create or manage resources across units that will give birth to networked cohesion. When the center has granted autonomy to the periphery, everything possible must be done in order to create common values. Within the network company, the units must learn both the necessity of having mutual confidence and a cross-cutting awareness of their interdependencies.

Besides the norm of reciprocity and the importance of trust, it seems important to clarify a few points concerning the way in which the network is activated as an organizational mode. What are the operating principles, and in particular, how are decisions made concerning the entire network? In this respect, publications on the theme of the network are rather evasive. Concrete answers to these questions need to be provided. Once the idea of operating without formal hierarchy is accepted, it is necessary to analyze in detail the way in which the interactions between peripheral units contribute to the creation of organizational cohesion. This thought process can be started by analyzing research done on collegial organizations.

The collegial organization is a good example of a type of organization that operates essentially with the network as a basic principle. Lazega (1992) defines collegial organizations as organizations that gather together professionals (law firms, architectural firms, universities, professional bodies and groups, etc.). A reference to the ideal-typical definition of the collegial organization by Waters (1989) may be very useful. Its first characteristic is the exercise of authority that is based solely on competence. If the notion of competence is broadened to cover resources in general, we arrive at the existence of power within the network. However, this power is based solely on the resources held by the members of the organization (there is therefore no authority of the rational-legal type). The second principle is that of the 'company of equals.' No member is by nature superior to the others. They have the same status. This corresponds precisely to the logic of the network as a mode of organization. The third characteristic is the need for consensus; only a decision made unanimously or by the majority can be imposed upon all members and can have the weight of moral authority. Thus, the majority of collegial organizations operate on the basis of elected committees. Taking part in group decisions seems to be one of the key elements of collegial organizations, one that is often neglected by the network as an organizational mode and one that seems particularly important when this mode of organization is applied to the company.

Studies of company networks and collegiate organizations allow a better definition of the network as an organizational mode. Our objective will be to go further in this analysis and give substance to the network, in particular showing how the cohesion of a company can result from a cooperative and non-hierarchical approach among peripheral units. Before starting this empirical stage, however, we will clarify the positioning of this work once again by justifying in a precise manner our choice of the concept of mode of organization. The following section is devoted to this justification. This section concerns a rather academic debate and the reader who seeks a more concrete discussion may advance directly to the chapters that follow.

LIMITS TO THE CONFIGURATIONAL AND INSTITUTIONAL APPROACHES

The conceptual frame of reference in this work represents a real break in relation to the dominant theoretical approaches which concern new organizational forms. Yet this conceptual framework is the only one that can bring about a real advance in our understanding of these complex phenomena.

Two different angles are often taken in order to explain the evolution towards new organizational forms. The first approach is that of configurations. Though conceptually very rich, study in terms of configurations has often been limited by the simplistic applications which have been used. The multiplicity of forms found within companies gives a clear advantage to the concept of mode of organization. The same conclusions can be drawn about the institutional approach, which does not allow us to understand why one institution is better than another in carrying out certain transactions and especially what are the limitations of this superiority (for example, when the firm borrows from the market or the network).

The Configurational Approach

The configurational approach is widespread in the study of new organizational forms. It generally focuses on the definition of a new organizational model by induction or even by taking inspiration from already completed work. This procedure is very useful in the discovery stage for the first analysis of a reality which is viewed as complex because it is a new field of research. However, the multiplicity of configurations thus obtained and presented systematically as hard-and-fast models spreads confusion and makes any consensus impossible. The richness and subtlety of organizational reality is difficult to summarize in a limited number of summary configurations. Postulating the existence of organizational configurations does not in any way imply that it is possible or even interesting to itemize all the existing configurations; this approach is much too simplistic and does not allow us to progress.

Configurations, archetypes or gestalts

The configurational approach is based on the idea that not all the possible combinations of attributes exist. The attributes therefore have the tendency to 'fall' into coherent configurations. The attributes are interdependent, and this interdependence can only be understood globally. A configuration can be defined as: 'any multidimensional constellation of conceptually distinct characteristics that commonly occur together. Numerous dimensions of environments, industries, technologies, strategies, structures, cultures, ideologies, groups, members, processes, practices, beliefs, and outcomes have been said to cluster into configurations, archetypes, or gestalts' (Meyer, Tsui and Hinings 1993, p 1175).

The first principle of configurations is therefore their discontinuous character: not all combinations of attributes are viable. A number of endogenous and exogenous explanations can be called on to explain this phenomenon. The exogenous factors essentially correspond to the selection made by the environment – in accordance with the hypotheses of the ecology of populations – which determines which configurations are viable. The endogenous factors correspond to a variety of mimetic and normative behaviors, as well as the use of coercive power by some institutional actors, which tends to produce some standardization of models.

The second important principle of configurations is the evolution by jumps ('saltus') of one configuration into another. This brings into contrast two conceptions of the evolution of organizational forms: Darwinism and saltationism. The Darwinian approach hypothesizes the existence of discrete changes, of mutations that explain a progressive evolution. Nevertheless, this theory does not allow for an explanation of certain revolutions in existing species. The hypothesis of the existence of leaps between distinct forms has therefore been introduced. In this way, any given configuration can be modified and continuously adapted, but only within a certain limit. Beyond this limit, the schema of contingency and its underlying linear nature no longer apply. Once the limit of a given configuration is reached, the full equilibrium of the configuration is called into question. Interdependence between components is such that the modification of one element beyond this limit leads to a complete restructuring of the system.

The configurational approach is very rich; it allows one to understand the cohesion of an organization from a different and overall perspective. However, it often serves as a premature justification for simplistic approaches that are not implied by its basic postulates. Mintzberg (1989) uses the configurational approach and justifies resorting to a small number of configurations by the need to grasp the organizational form or 'gestalt' in its entirety and to understand interactions from an overall perspective and not element by element. It is indeed important to recognize the interdependence of organizational elements. On the other hand, it seems unlikely that the multiplicity of organizational forms can be grasped from five basic models, and a review of Mintzberg's publications confirms this point of view. In 1979, there were five organizational forms (the simple structure, the mechanical bureaucracy, the professional bureaucracy, the divisional form, and the adhocracy), unless the two variants of adhocracy are counted, making a total of six. A seventh (or eighth) form was also described: the missionary configuration. The missionary configuration went on to receive its pedigree alongside the political organization (Mintzberg 1989). The question that remains is this: are there five, six, seven, eight, or nine configurations? In any case, not one more! Mintzberg's contribution is obvious, and the objective here is not at all to call into question the interest of this type of approach, but rather to show its limits (limits that are even more pronounced because we are currently witnessing a multiplication of possible forms rather than an alignment of a few unique models). It therefore seems very difficult to describe this diversity by means of simplistic typologies, even more so because they conceal a more complex reality than the configurational approach can allow. Configurations certainly have pedagogical value, and up to now they have allowed us to forge a model of what the new organizational forms are. But it is now necessary to go further.

The different logics of hybridization

If one wishes to maintain a configurational concept of organization while being aware of the multiplicity of organizational forms, it is necessary to reconsider the way in which hybridization between the proposed models is conceived. This leads us directly to take account of principles with ideal-typical properties, the modes of organization, and to attempt to identify the compatibilities and incompatibilities between these major principles. In this way we can reach a more subtle level of analysis, a level that allows for deeper understanding of the multiplicity of organizational forms whilst at the same time remembering that it is impossible to accept every one of them.

It is indeed possible to push the analysis further by questioning the status of the configurations already present in the literature of strategic management. Doty, Glick and Huber (1993) propose a thorough and detailed analysis that is based on the concept of the ideal-type. Etymologically, the type is an imprint; therefore, the ideal-type is an imprint, an ideal representation of reality. The entire question of the status of configurations lies in the two meanings that can be given to the word ideal: ideal, as in a configuration that would exist only in our imagination, or ideal, as in a perfect configuration towards which one must strive. Therefore, the question is to know whether the configurations are models that must be adopted as far as possible or whether they are models that hold up only insofar as we are aware that reality mixes the models so as to produce hybrid configurations. Following this line it is possible to envisage four types of hybridization.

In the first type, there is no hybridization possible between ideals. The viability of an organization depends on how close it can be brought to that of an ideal-type. For the organization, it is therefore necessary to try to get as close as possible to one of the ideal configurations.

In the second concept, that of the contingent ideal-type, environmental variables are placed by themselves on the one hand, while strategic and structural variables are placed by themselves on the other. Environmental variables can vary continuously, while configurations are shown discontinuously on the strategic and structural axis. The environmental variables are therefore contingent factors whose combination imposes the choice of structure-strategy configuration. Thus, these are discontinuous models, each point appropriate to a particular context.

The third concept is that of the hybrid-contingent type in which each combination of contingent factors requires a particular combination of strategy-structure configurations. Hybridization is thus possible, but it is strictly constrained by contingent factors.

The last model is the hybrid type in which many hybridizations are possible in a given context.

The multitude of new organizational forms encountered and the diversity of the principles that organize them impel us to consider this last model, the hybrid type. At first glance, this model might seem to contradict the configurational approach: if a multitude of hybridizations is possible, the idea of configuration no longer means anything. In fact, the idea that we seek to emphasize is instead one of equifinality: there exists a plurality of viable forms in any given context. This does not imply that all forms are viable, and therefore the idea of configuration remains. Additionally, the elements on which the concept of hybridization is founded are not ideal-types in the sense of an ideal that one must endeavor to reach: we cannot construct such models. Rather, existing configurations are combinations of a certain number of elementary dimensions with ideal-typical properties that we shall attempt to demonstrate: we refer here to modes of organization. Instead of proposing model configurations disconnected from organizational reality, we are interested in proposing modes of organization that allow a better understanding of the multiplicity of existing forms.

The Institutional Approach of Transaction Cost Theory

The special characteristics of the case of the institutional approach, as has been developed by Williamson, clearly show the pertinence of analysis in terms of modes of organization. Indeed, recourse to organizational modes is the only method that allows the results of the economic model of transaction costs to be justified and, ultimately, that allows theory to evolve in the light of the recent changes in the internal organization of companies.

Transaction cost theory is principally concerned with the study of two alternative institutions: the market and the hierarchy (Williamson 1975). The market is appropriate in cases of transactions that use non-specific assets, while the hierarchy is suitable in cases that use mixed and idiosyncratic assets. Thus the unit of analysis is, on the one hand, the transaction (or a collection of transactions that have the same characteristics) and, on the other hand, the institution that is best suited to dealing with this transaction (the market or the hierarchy). Thus recourse to a suitably adapted institution is needed to justify transaction cost theory. The differences between institutions lie essentially in the type of contract that governs them and in the structures affected if there are lawsuits (Williamson 1991).

If analysis stops at this level, it is difficult to account for the fact that the majority of transactions are actually a mix of market and hierarchy. In fact, it is not because there is recourse to an institution of a particular type that transaction costs are reduced. Rather, it is because market and bureaucracy are combined in an optimal manner as modes of organization when the institution deals with the transaction.

Transaction cost theory is in fact based on the idea of modes of organization, but this essential intermediary is not placed at the heart of the analysis. Indeed, if it can be considered that the market is the institution that is best adapted for certain transactions, it is because of its ability to bring strong incentives to bear on the actors at the smallest cost. As for the company, it is best suited to implement a system of weak incentives. This type of system does not permit the actors to internalize the organizational objectives. An audit system therefore has to be put into place. However, the analysis of incentives is treated quickly by Williamson and he does not give an account of the way in which institutions can operate between market and hierarchy (i.e. by combining both organizational modes, the market and the bureaucracy) or of the method by which a company can use (or not use) the market as an organizational mode. Williamson himself recognizes this limit and the importance of this problem in his theory: ' . in ternal organization is unable to replicate the high-powered incentives of markets and is subject to bureaucratic disabilities. The factors that lie behind those conditions, however, are hardly touched upon. The ways in which firms can improve their incentive and bureaucratic competences in relation to markets also warrant more self-conscious attention' (Williamson, 1985, p 403).

Because transaction cost theory neglects the notion of modes of organization and continues to reason in terms of institutions, the usefulness of this theory is considerably limited if we seek to understand the institutions of capitalism. In order to advance, it seems essential to examine the way in which modes of organization can be used in a given type of institution.[22] We look particularly at the case of the company. After illustrating the possibilities of the network (Chapter 3), we try to analyze and understand better the concrete mechanisms by which the company can put this organizational mode into practice. The subsequent chapters deal with this question first by showing the possibilities of transfers and collaborative projects between peripheral units without the intervention of the center (Chapter 4) and then by studying the composition of a community of exchange between such units (Chapter 5).

22. As argued by Foss: 'One solution is to keep the traditional firm–market distinction, for example, on legal grounds, but supplement it with a more refined taxonomy of the many different coordination mechanisms that may be implemented inside the traditional governance structures. In such a perspective [•] new organizational forms represent not so much a blurring of the boundaries between traditional governance structures *per se*, as an increasing use of coordination mechanisms traditionally characteristic of one structure inside another structure' (2002, p. 5).

3. Creating a space of freedom

The primary characteristic of the network organization is the absence of formal hierarchy. Strong autonomy is therefore allowed to the peripheral units. This autonomy gives the peripheral units a unique free space within which they can develop their own strategies. This room for maneuver is one of the essential factors that pushes the evolution of companies towards an organization based more on the network. It opens up various possibilities. Some of these are connected to cost savings, but others aim especially at improving their agility. One of the network's first effects on both the central and peripheral workforce is the start of an era of 'light' structures. Further, it is clear that what is being sought here is flexibility rather than cost savings. Flexibility and agility in structures lead to competitive advantages that are at the heart of companies' strategies. They can push a company's relationships with customers well beyond what was possible under more hierarchical structures. The room for maneuver which they give to companies lies also at the origin of innovations based on experience in the field and in customer relations.

From this first analysis, development of structures emerges as a key element of strategy. Organization thus becomes an essential dimension for achieving competitive advantage. This competitive advantage will also emerge from analysis of the other essential dimension of the network: a form of cooperative cross-cutting organization that will be discussed in the two chapters that follow. It is indeed essential not to lose sight of the fact that the autonomy which peripheral units enjoy can be disruptive for a company. Yet the network is more than this; it is also a factor conducive to cohesion

SIMPLIFIED STRUCTURES

The first effect of autonomy is the simplification of structures. For more than a decade now, we have been accustomed to slimmed-down holding companies, those simplified head offices that see their workforces reduced from several thousand to some hundred or even down to a mere dozen people. The lightness of these central structures is an important point of departure for the development of increased autonomy. In certain companies that we have researched, we shall see that this autonomy can be pushed rather a long way. It is also important to note the slimming-down of peripheral structures. This arises both from links with central units that have become less restrictive and also from the desire to guarantee permanent flexibility and adaptability.

Minimalist Central Structures

An important step in the evolution towards a network organization is certainly the simplification of central structures. This simplification clearly has an advantage in terms of cost, but it is not to this advantage that actors give priority. The simplification of central structures appears above all as a necessary condition for the functioning of the network. The real autonomy of peripheral units is possible only if the central workforce is not large. Directors and functional managers are even less tempted to exercise a hierarchical hold over peripheral units if they do not have the human resources to do so. That is how groups like Colas can have headquarters which contain only about one hundred people.

The group that has pushed the logic of simplified structures the furthest is certainly the GTIE Group. This organization is made up of three 'management poles' that are divided according to geographic and industrial criteria.[23] The Group's General Management is made up of the Managing Directors of the three poles, which remain legally independent, as well as the Managing Director of the GTIE pole. Then, for each pole, the executive committee includes its chairperson, one or several general managers and deputy general managers, a financial director, a certain number of regional directors and, for GTIE itself, the director of technical and commercial development. The only functional support, apart from the financial function, is given by the marketing director and the technical and commercial development director for the GTIE pole, as well as a central Innovation and Development Unit. The Innovation and Development Unit ensures that the company keeps up with leading edge technology; it can also initiate the development of specific techniques. These developments can then be entrusted to companies within the group. The Finance Department designs and monitors the management system. This department also intervenes to support companies in various fields, but it does not possess the power of injunction. Because the regional managers are in charge of a certain number of 'companies,' they make up an intermediate management level between the center and peripheral units, and they coordinate the activity in given zones or trades. In a situation in which functional departments are almost non-existent,

---

23. See Appendix I for more detail on the structure of the four firms studied.

the regional directors undertake very broad monitoring of the companies' activities. However, it is very clear that the large number of units under a regional director's responsibility makes detailed monitoring by function impossible. The simplified central structure thus emerges as a guarantee of the frugality with which the central and intermediary management are able to intervene.

However, in other situations there is a whole series of resources which are best concentrated within the same entity. This does not necessarily imply a functional department with formal hierarchical power. Thus, Air Liquide often chooses to transform some of its departments into peripheral support units. These support units serve the regions (the regions themselves look after marketing and a part of production). This type of organization makes it possible to achieve flexible functioning that is based on mutual adjustment, without introducing a central coordination unit. One particularly vivid example of this is the development resources, both human and material, which are made available to the regions. In France, these resources are concentrated within two Centers of Expertise in Procedures, Installation, and Application (CEPIA). These two CEPIAs group together specialists in all possible uses of air gases, but these specialists do not intervene in a centralized way as would a development department. If a region needs a particular development, it calls on the resources of the CEPIAs, whose task is to provide services for the regions. A similar way of working is found in the present relationship between the Floxal teams and the regions[24] for the installation of production units on the customers' sites.

CFDP has chosen a different solution to avoid the proliferation of the functional workforce: outsourcing. All the functions that require real specialists are outsourced. Former employees who no longer have a place within the new simplified structure are encouraged and even helped to become self-employed if they so desire: 'Everything that we do not know how to do is done outside the company, rather than by centralized departments. For example, information technology is now completely subcontracted; nothing is done internally anymore.' The managers preferred less organized, autonomous individuals to centralized departments. This idea was reaffirmed by the Inter-regional Committee which used the following argument: 'Someone who is merely functional does not know the clients, which is not good. It gives him a vision which is too limited.' An interesting link is thus established between outsourcing and reduced intervention by the center. By abolishing central departmental intermediaries, outsourcing allows a company to limit the risk of a return to hierarchy.

---

24. For a detailed account of the role of Floxal teams, see Chapter 4 on common projects.

Flexible Peripheral Units

The same concern for simplification is found for peripheral units as for
central ones. The flexibility and adaptability which result from this
simplification are considered to be essential sources of competitive
advantage. The simplification of central structures takes on even more
importance from this point of view. Indeed, this simplification not only
guarantees the autonomy of peripheral units but also permits a reduction in
the reporting requirements for all functions, beginning with a reduction of the
workforce of the peripheral structure itself. This makes it possible to avoid
having the intermediate departments which are characteristic of bloated
multidivisional firms and allows the size of peripheral units to be reduced.

In the four cases studied, the small size of units is seen as an essential
element. The size of the units studied lies between less than ten people for the
smallest teams at CFDP and around 120 people for the largest units in other
cases. The reduced size for a specific project is clearly one of the important
elements of network organization: the goal is to obtain a flexible organization
that is adaptable and that listens to its local customers. Reduced size can also
be associated with enhanced motivation for individuals, who are given
greater responsibility.

For example, at GTIE, forming small units is viewed as an essential
determinant of performance: 'People feel and perform better in small units;
they are happier and more efficient (if they are happy, they are more
efficient). Responsibility must be delegated as much as possible.' Following
this way of thinking, the sizes of Air Liquide's regions have been reduced
voluntarily in order to maintain the group's flexibility and ability to react.
Some people would like to see sizes reduced even more: 'There are
mechanical limits to the size of the regions. Nantes (70 people) is too big.
The optimal size lies between 30 and 40 people.'

The control of size requires a smaller competitive field. GTIE, for example,
does not hesitate systematically to split a company that has more than one
strategic project: the diversity of projects limits the company's ability to
listen and the will needed to successfully complete the projects in question.
Size is thus seen as a problem which finds its solution by fragmenting a
company as soon as the coexistence of two strategic projects is perceived
within it: 'In general, when there is a problem of size, the real problem is that
there are several projects.' The case of Générale d'Infographie is a good
illustration of the logic of fragmentation. The company was created on the
basis of Computer-Aided Design (CAD) activities. This company developed
and grew, and its size quickly exceeded 50 people. It then appeared that there
were two sub-activities within the company: one for the local groups and one
for industries. Two companies were therefore created (with the same legal

structure), and they now each develop their projects independently. Thanks to this fragmentation, 'the group started expanding once again, whilst we had been having some difficulties before.'

Similarly, to get the most out of network organizations, it is important that this autonomy be continued at the level of internal organization in the units. A non-hierarchical and cooperative structure must therefore be created within the peripheral units. The internal organization of Air Liquide's regions is without a doubt one of the best examples. The director of each region is in effect the only person who has a hierarchical link with all of the personnel in that region. There are some 'experts' or 'guarantors,' but they no longer have a hierarchical role. This absence of hierarchical links is largely seen as a trump card for the adaptation and flexibility of a unit. As one operator said: 'No time is wasted in passing along of information. There aren't any hierarchical links with the company's engineer. If there is a technical problem, I go to see him; it's important that it isn't the bosses who facilitate the contact. Everything goes just fine; there isn't any sign of the boss, so relationships are friendly, which is nicer.'

One final point may be important for the better response to local customers' expectations: the possibility of adapting the structure of peripheral units to their activities. This need was felt essentially within GTIE, where the peripheral units did not all do the same job. In this group, the fixed structures are adapted for each company to the type of customer envisaged for it. Again, the example of Générale d'Infographie is interesting in this respect. The 'network and community' company[25] is present at four different sites in France, whereas the 'specialized information system' company is found at only one site: 'The people from Network and Community are constrained to have a local presence because they must offer services from nearby. We are concentrated in one place because we work with important, large accounts.'

OPEN BOUNDARIES

Adaptability and flexibility are thus the key words for autonomous peripheral units that depend on a slimmed-down center. The actors regularly justify this ability to adapt in terms of their readiness to serve their customers. The essential objective is to improve the service provided. Companies must be able to do things better and tailor their services to the needs of local

---

25. 'Entreprise collectivités et réseaux', dealing with the networks of local communities such as town, district councils,... the specialized information system company has corporate clients.

customers who have their own particular demands. It seems that, if we take this one step further, the units are placed literally under the control of the customer, sometimes even in a formal manner, as in the case of CFDP.

Local Relationships

The development of local relationships aims above all at improving the service provided to customers while being able to identify new needs. The customer is thus placed at the heart of the peripheral units. This means that every individual in the peripheral units, not only those who exercise a commercial function, must be concerned with customer relations. Beyond this direct relationship with the customer, the actors in peripheral units must integrate themselves completely into the local environment.

This quasi-obsession with customer relations is very evident within GTIE. As in the other cases, the strategic plan of each of GTIE's companies is often centered on a particular geographic zone, with a limited number of clients, and working generally within areas that are limited. In order to promote the idea of the importance of customer relations internally, the metaphor of an inverted pyramid is used: 'The logic is that of an inverted pyramid, with the customer as the originating point of that pyramid. Companies must be close to the customer, both geographically and culturally.'

If the operation of GTIE's customer relations is analyzed in more detail, we find that everything is done to ensure that all members of the company are concerned with customer relations. The goal is both to enable a daily follow-up and to develop a strategic perspective on the relationship. The first contact with the customer is through the Account Manager: he makes sure that the contact is followed up and developed for each particular project. However, for most activities, there is intervention at the customer's own site, in which case the technicians there play an essential part in the interface: 'There is a follow-up meeting on site by the project leader and the assembling technician, and that must go well. We [the Account Managers] intervene in a much more pointed way, we talk about other things, the future...' It is therefore important that everyone have access to customer information: 'Everyone is familiar with the files. Everyone has access to the information, and that is the best way to give responsibility to the individual players.[...]The technicians have to know the customer and have links with him.'

Customer relations are considered to be one of GTIE's key advantages. They are one of the elements that is taken directly into account when defining the key strategic directions for the group. The companies of the group generally seek out activities in which very close proximity to the client is possible: 'The fact that we have entered the automation business allows us to develop as second level subcontractors. In relations to our electrical integration trade we have nothing to do with the user. With automation, we are in direct contact with the customer.' It thus becomes possible to propose joint supply activities with former customers (first-level subcontractors), who may become subcontractors (second-level) for certain operations. Thus, the transition from electrical integration to data processing has become one of the important strategic directions for the group.

Similarly, at Air Liquide they insist strongly that all actors from peripheral units must be involved directly in relationships with customers. At the core of these relationships are the members of the commercial structure: commercial executives (administrative functions), account executives (technical functions), and sales representatives (strictly commercial functions) who work as a troika to develop relations with a group of customers. Each one establishes strong relationships within his area of expertise with the main customers, including the administrative functions. As one commercial executive said,: 'We know some clients very, very well. We go and see the accounting people at least once a year. Even if there is not a problem, we go and see people because everything goes much better after that.' The idea behind these special relationships is to create a relationship that is stronger than a simple commercial one: 'The commercial executive's relationships with the customers encompass both technical and commercial subjects as far as installations are concerned. The purpose is to give information and a little advice. The greater goal is that when they need something, they will buy it from Air Liquide.' Sales are still a central concern, but with the prospect of partnership and enlarged service: 'The relationship is more a partnership than a purely sales relationship. It is about getting the customer to become a partner, giving service rather than selling him molecules of gas. The relationship should continue into the long term.'

In general, all regional members are likely to devote their energies to the customer and to customer service. This is the case for the regional manager, who guarantees the development of relations with strategic clients: 'The regional manager has a very strong commercial function. He is a salesperson.' The heads of development (R&D intermediaries) also take part in this commercial approach and go into the field with the sales representatives in case technical questions associated with the use of the gases arise. On a less regular basis, anyone can be called upon to carry out these commercial functions; for example, a security coordinator: 'At the request of sales managers, I did customer promotions. In such cases, I go alone in order to carry out a security demonstration, the sales manager makes an offer and it's invoiced.' More informally, a park operator told us that he often answered questions asked by the customers through their chauffeurs.

The social capital developed by a company can also be directed towards other actors and have an indirect effect on customer relations. A group of actors who are particularly relevant for the development of sales are the companies that market the equipment necessary for using gas, like welding equipment. Relations with such companies are handled in effect by the heads of development, so that some of them sign agreements with the companies which give them 'information payments' if they give information which leads to business such that a gas supply contract is obtained.'

A concern for local involvement is also central to the choices made by Colas, as far as structure is concerned. A similar competitive advantage arises by establishing privileged ties with local customers. In particular, its agencies must be able to play a truly advisory role beyond that of merely responding to invitations to tender. This involvement in the local milieu goes much further than a simple commercial approach: it is not about merely selling a product, but rather about being present on the spot. This is why the large majority of the personnel in the agencies are recruited from within the region. Agency heads and foremen must be local people of weight who participate in the life of the community. Many actors at all levels of the organization insist on the importance of the local involvement of the agency. The contacts with local actors are essential to its performance: 'A fundamental point is integration into the local fabric through permanent contact with the key people there,' 'Relationships are important: you have to go to make contact,' 'A civil engineering firm should be considered as a confederation of local businesses: most of the personnel are of local origin, and the same should be true for the purchases of material inputs.' The idea that business be local is firmly anchored.

The creation of a Unit for Major Works that undertakes very large construction projects at the regional level illustrates this concern well. Indeed, the risk is that local agencies managers may abandon their own customer base for the large but short-lived construction projects: 'For very large projects, if they are undertaken locally, it is to the detriment of other activities that the agency manager neglects'; 'If the agencies dedicate themselves to the construction of major infrastructure in their area, they neglect the clients who are the basis of their business.'

Towards Control by the Customers?

Thus, one of the desired characteristics when setting up autonomous units is clearly their adaptation to the demands of local customers. The first step is to establish ties with them and to adapt the company's supply to their particular needs. It is essential to understand that the results of this approach go well beyond commercial matters. Analysis in depth shows clearly that the customer has a very strong impact on all the decisions made by peripheral units. So one may ask whether it is desirable to go even further, as CFDP did, by opening the boundaries of the company completely to its customers.

Social networks analysis[26] has shown itself particularly useful in highlighting the nature of these well-established relationships with customers. It is only by analyzing sociometric information that we become aware of the importance of the role played by customers with regard to the peripheral units. For the four cases studied, the ties that exist with customers affect a number of actors equivalent to or greater than the total of those existing with the center of the group. Most striking are the results concerning the networks of control. We can also note that even more agents indicate that their actions are directly or indirectly controlled by the customers than by the center of the group: network functioning thus fulfils its role well, in that it puts the customer at the center of the peripheral units. There is indeed development towards a real external control that is coming to replace internal control: the customers contribute directly to the coherent development of the group as a whole through the pressure that they exert on the peripheral units. This development arises from the need to respond directly to the expectations of the customers by adapting supply to the needs of the local base and by combining additional services with the basic service which is supplied. In this way, the network puts itself at the service of the company's customers. It is interesting to note that only methods such as those used in the research for this book allow this kind of information to come to light. With the exception of CFDP's case, in which these developments had been taken a very long way, the agents were not necessarily aware of this phenomenon.

Why shouldn't this course of action be pushed even further? CFDP chose to do it by bringing insurance intermediaries[27] – the customers of the company – into all company meetings and all collective decisions. Since 1993, the insurance intermediaries have participated systematically in all team meetings: each delegate comes with one or several 'partners.' This participation of the intermediaries was put into place progressively and has now become standard throughout the company. The make-up of the teams often proved to be difficult, at least at the start: 'It took us two years to create our team because we had such different ways of thinking in the beginning. People are used to working all alone and do not know how to work in teams.' The presence of the insurance intermediaries enabled teams to progress more

---

26. The tools used are presented in Appendix II. It can just briefly be recalled that social network analysis is used to analyze inter-individual links. Such an analysis was conducted for several sub-units in each firm.
27. Insurance intermediaries can be either independent insurance brokers or independent agents. The agents distribute the products of one company only as the brokers select the best offer for their clients.

rapidly through the issues raised and to refocus the discussions: 'The objective is the following: the company must have its roots in its customers. The more a decision comes from a customer, the better it will be.' The presence of intermediaries allows the teams systematically to refocus their debates onto the themes that are important for them. Furthermore, they can influence the choices made. In effect, in the team, all the delegates have the same status; the status of customer gives the intermediaries legitimacy, which makes it easier to take decisions: they are really listened to. Some of the intermediaries seem to be interested in having a forum for discussion and for sharing of problems; others subscribe more particularly to a philosophy, an original approach to management. The setting-up of dual teams is the result of a long process that the company went through between 1989 and 1993. Through these experiences, the need for a structure of exchange with the independent insurance intermediaries became obvious, but an efficient way for this structure to work was found only thanks to the presence of customers.

It is obvious that it is not always possible to give all the information about a company to its clients. However, the approach taken by CFDP fits directly into the logic of opening companies' boundaries to customers. In order to obtain these results, CFDP to break down a certain number of barriers which were essentially psychological, and there is much to make one think that such barriers are solidly entrenched in a large company. However, the approach can inspire change and is directly in line with the argument of this chapter: the fact that the customer plays a very strong role in peripheral units. Without going as far as an opening of boundaries as marked at that of CFDP, dialogue with customers would undoubtedly be enriched by opportunities for more formal and more frequent joint reflection.

INNOVATION

Innovation in the field is one of the most notable results of the establishment of autonomous peripheral units. The creation of a space of freedom is absolutely necessary, making use of the capacity for local innovation. Moreover, such innovations are even more pertinent to the group's development because they are designed by operational personnel, often in close collaboration with the customers. Whether they apply to new services, new or modified products, or to an aspect of marketing or organization, these innovations in the field can very often be transposed to the rest of the group. It is in any case systematic for all practical purposes in structures which are organized by geographical division. It is thus important to note from now on the significance of the cooperative and cross-cutting approach for the diffusion and improvement of these innovations within a firm as a whole. We shall develop this in the chapters which follow.

Autonomy and Innovation

The capacity for innovation that peripheral units can display is directly linked to their degree of autonomy. If the products, the associated services and the methods of organization are set by central management, the absence of sufficient room for maneuver left to peripheral units can only limit their capacity for innovation. On the other hand, the freedom which they enjoy under the network organization allows their learning ability to remain unscathed, and this learning opens the way to propositions that may be useful at the local level or on the scale of the group as a whole. In this way, they go well beyond the flexible adaptation of standard supply to local conditions.

Innovation is clearly one of the points that was put forward to justify the reform of Air Liquide's structures. The resulting advantage shows itself in the field in concrete terms and is well perceived at head office: 'The structure by regions is less efficient as far as production is concerned, but it brings about new developments.' The approach visibly bears fruit, and the proof is in the constant innovation in the field. Autonomous innovations can affect every element of the Air Liquide supply: 'There are more and more innovative structures and leaps forward in the field. Innovations can apply to new services, to new product uses, to new products or to other ways of capturing new clients. There are many new products which are being created in the regions on the foundation of the national rules.'

One characteristic example is that of adapting the 'telemetry' system of measurement at a distance, to the stocks of gas cylinders. Air Liquide set up a real-time information system called DATAL. The system is used to monitor the level of gas in the customers' tanks. It thus became possible to restock the cryogenic tanks as soon as is necessary and without the need for the customer to worry about it. Furthermore, this new system made it easier to schedule deliveries in a way which was more appropriate. This outcome, greatly appreciated by the customers, was possible only for the large tanks and not for stocks of cylinders. Thanks to a magnetic card, a regional team was able to keep track of the use of cylinders by customers. The service provided for the replenishment of stocks of liquid gas could therefore be adapted to the delivery of refilled cylinders, which allowed stocks to be optimized. In this case, innovation carried out by a region had worldwide consequences for the group.

In another region, a customized labeling system carried out by the team who put together orders allows a certain amount of information to be transmitted directly in the course of delivery. Those who put the orders together can thus label cylinders directly and on site with information that is specific to the order being prepared. The innovations which emanate from the field are in large part publicized by organizing an innovation forum, or in *Initiatives*, the journal of the Industrial Gas Services department.

Similarly, CFDP emphasizes strong autonomy in order to encourage local innovation. Thus, there are few 'products' at CFDP. There are standard contracts, but representatives are free to make special contracts in order to respond to the expectations of the insurance intermediaries. These contracts are created by the delegates themselves with no specific authorization from the center. Their room for maneuver is truly very important since 'each delegate makes the decisions for his sector. This is also true for contracts. There is a standard contract whose general characteristics are defined. Nevertheless, each delegate makes special contracts if he wants, and everyone does it.' 'We don't know all our contracts; everyone develops the contracts that he wants. This freedom produces capacity for innovation never before seen in the world of insurance.' This very free approach to custom-written contracts represents a total break with that approach adopted by traditional insurance companies in which the insurance intermediary must first sell a contract to a customer and then get it accepted by several departments in the company. Such a system makes any modification or adjustment very difficult. For some of the large clients, claim payments are sometimes made even if the client is not covered by a guarantee, which is a completely new approach in the insurance world.

As well as the innovation in the contracts themselves, the autonomy given to the delegates allows constant adaptation to the intermediaries' needs and strong innovation in that area. The objective of each delegate is thus to help the insurance intermediaries in all areas that can be useful to them: 'The insurance intermediary is always alone. In the sales representative, he finds a partner who accompanies him without seeking any direct interest. The interest comes later.' Therein lies a unique characteristic of CFDP's approach. In traditional firms, new services are invoiced to customers and the objective is even to invoice them for more as a result of these new services. In CFDP's case, services are not invoiced; this is the condition necessary to maintain an SME in a competitive environment made up of much larger companies. CFDP delegates go as far as setting up a point for legal information at their customers' branches, assuring a permanent presence for CFDP and training collaborators at the branch office. Organizational audits also take place in order to give intermediaries the opportunity to improve the way their branches operate. Representatives have been recruited with this in mind, for the majority of them were formerly consultants, not jurists.

Innovation in Customer Contact

What makes the innovations carried out by peripheral units so rich is the privileged relationship that they establish with their customers. In this analysis of innovation, it is the importance of customer relations which sets the direction for innovation in the field. This innovation work with customers can go as far as to make it necessary to create mixed ad hoc structures in which the company, the customer and sometimes other partners all take part. The case of GTIE's vertical partnerships which operate at different levels of subcontracting has already been discussed. However, it is once again CFDP that goes a very long way in this direction by giving total freedom to its delegates in such matters.

There is no limit a priori to what representatives can do for an insurance intermediary. Every initiative taken with an intermediary is viewed as heading in the right direction, particularly if it leads to a project in direct association with this intermediary. Among the numerous examples of innovation has been the creation in association with brokers and lawyers of a telephone service which provides legal assistance for small businesses. Another project goes even further: an independent venture has been set up including both CFDP delegates and intermediaries. In effect, a company independent of CFDP was set up with four brokers and four delegates in order to develop a new service. This service made it easier for the brokers to reissue renewal notices. Companies always send off renewal notices to insured parties. However, some brokers prefer to send personalized notices that allow them to reinforce their image and pass on contingent messages. A simpler way was needed to reissue notices. So the eight brokers and delegates bought some equipment together and created a separate company. 'This poses no problem as far as CFDP is concerned, even if they become managers of this company and make a profit from it. If the development of delegates takes place by creating a company that can make a profit, why not? The limit is that of the service given to the broker.'

These types of developments and innovations are only possible insofar as strong links of trust are established between the insurance intermediaries and the CFDP delegates. The same is true for projects which include competitors or subcontractors at different levels. The social capital developed through relationships by the peripheral unit is therefore an essential trump card that makes sure that innovation directed towards the client takes place, innovation that includes the most appropriate partners.

4. The first cross-cutting steps

This chapter is the first of two that analyze the concrete mechanisms by which peripheral units can mobilize the network as a mode of organization. The chapter begins with a description of the autonomous interactions that affect specific points where a mutual interest is clearly identified and whose effects can be seen in the relatively short term. These transfers and collaborative projects are characterized by their concrete nature. They fall directly within the field of the daily preoccupations of people in the units, which leads naturally to the involvement of the workers concerned.

The transfers may be of means − loans of equipment, exchanges of teams − or of projects that do not have repercussions for the structures of the units. In these cases of relatively well-signposted coordination, the interaction between the peripheral units does not pose any particular problem. Everyone can see clearly in the short term what the mutual interest in the transaction is. The redivision of roles is therefore simple, and direct interaction between units occurs in a natural way, sometimes even standardized by means of the tools of information technology.

On the other hand, for more complex operations or in situations where the immediate outcomes are unclear, units experience greater difficulties in working together. This is especially true when it comes to canvassing clients and for collaborative projects which require the recombination of structures. Canvassing a shared clientele requires strong involvement from all the units concerned, for outcomes which require cooperation that goes beyond a bilateral framework and concerns all the peripheral units. Projects that require the recombination of structures are subject to important functional constraints which can limit their long-term impact.

TRANSFERS BETWEEN UNITS

There are several cases in which sub-units carry out some simple transfer operations directly. In the companies studied, this arises most often with exchanges of equipment and teams, product sales, and in some cases, transfers of customers. It seems that exchanges of teams and equipment do not pose any particular problem. They can be managed easily between units acting autonomously, through meetings and by electronic means. They are especially necessary in cyclical activities, when units can find themselves in very different local circumstances: some in periods of overload and others underloaded. In the same way, adjustments linked to product transfers between units are managed directly. These require cooperation, as there is the risk that each of the units might formulate unrealistic and unfounded demands. Collaborative management of certain customers does not pose any particular problem.

On the other hand, canvassing other units' customers does not just happen by itself, even in another zone or in a different trade. In fact, there are three main reasons which explain this difficulty: the idea of each unit's individual turf, the fear of another unit's failure, and the contingent nature of the reciprocity of the entire operation. It seems that the success of this type of operation is subject to the fact that the actors in both units know each other and already trust each other. Table 4.1 summarizes the conclusions concerning transfers between units.

Table 4.1 Transfers between units

DIMENSION	OBJECTIVES	LIMITS
Simple transfers	• Irregularity of the activity	• Protection of resources
Product sales	• Vertical integration	• Production on the national scale
		• Unrealistic demands
Canvassing Customers	• Enlarged client base	• Turf
		• Fear of failure
		• Short-term vision

Simple transfers

In two of the cases studied (GTIE and Colas), the peripheral units had come to exchange equipment or teams on a more or less frequent basis. Transfers of equipment, teams or personnel have the same goal: to offset the periods of underload and of overload. In both companies, there is in effect a cyclical activity which affects zones within Colas' regions and trades within GTIE's companies, where the intensity of competition and the development of demand can be in sharp contrast with one another. In the two groups, there are units that experience an overload of work, while at the same time, there are others that do not have enough work. It is this irregularity in the level of activity that creates the need for exchange between units. In the cases of both

GTIE and Colas, these exchanges take place without the intervention of the center and do not seem to give rise to any particular problem.

For GTIE, companies within the same region come together periodically to discuss transfers of personnel for a given period. The group's activity is generally cyclical and is often governed by the results of invitations to tender. So there are often periods of underload followed by periods of overload. Exchanges of equipment or tools are made as needed. For the personnel out on site, there are monthly meetings within the different regions in order to evaluate needs. These meetings are run by someone from one of the companies. The people interviewed for the case studies indicated that the exchanges were 'very easy within the GTIE Group. Because of legal problems, things can be more tricky between subsidiaries.' The prices for exchanges of personnel are set at a predetermined internal rate, with no margin between one company and another. On this point, as for other aspects of cooperation between units within the group, 'there was a strong incentive at one stage, but understanding plays a role. There is not necessarily a financial incentive.'

Similarly, in the Colas Group, loans of equipment and exchanges of teams between agencies aim to offset possible slackening in activity. These exchanges are temporary and have the sole object of trying to avoid situations in which one team is not working or a piece of equipment is not being used in one agency when another agency is having to call on rental companies or to hire temporary workers. Certain specialized pieces of equipment are kept by particular agencies and their circulation has to be organized. All these exchanges are carried out autonomously and create no difficulties; as a result, contact remains very limited. The availability of stocks of equipment at the different centers are advertised on the computer network, which simplifies the transaction even more. Thus, thanks to the software, exchanges of equipment are very easy, even between agencies in different regions. Each agency's dispatchers gather information about availability, and make it accessible to all agencies. The BRIC software, which makes possible the exchanges of equipment between agencies, was created by the central IT department. The data is updated daily. The actors stress the simplicity of using the software: the data is available for consultation 'by all agency office managers or the dispatchers who then telephone each other to finalize the exchanges. In the case of specific equipment that is held only by certain agencies, the exchanges are carried out directly between the agencies. Everyone uses this system.' However, exchanges of teams, foremen, and regional managers are not organized systematically: 'If one site requires immediate attention (a last-minute unraveling of deals, or deals made which promise record speed) and all of the teams are busy, then neighboring agencies or subcontractors can be called in. It depends on the activity; last year, eight teams came to us from other agencies.'

Coordination between units does not therefore require any intervention from the center if it does not concern the creation of conditions of exchange (in the form of software, for example). Direct intervention by the center would most certainly be carried out in a heavy-handed way and give rise to problems of adjustment: local actors are best at foreseeing their own activity and carrying out adjustments. It is possible that units tend to limit exchanges in order not to let go of their equipment, thus protecting their own resources from the rest of the group. In our study we had no way to observe such a phenomenon; all the same, one can consider that this type of attitude would be still more marked in relation to a central body which managed all the exchanges, as opposed to the network organization, which, in a non-conflictual setting, has every chance of proving itself superior in such matters. Because the exchange in each case is carried out at cost, it is directly reflected by an improvement in the profit margin of each unit: the one does not have to bear the cost of unused resources, and the other benefits from conditions that are more advantageous than resorting to temporary workers or renting equipment. It is thus clear that it is in the best interests of both units to make as many exchanges as possible.

Product sales

Another type of relatively standardized transaction is that of product sales between peripheral units for which some units play the role of internal suppliers. In this section, we discuss sales of goods and services that do not require units to work together on a project. Among the four companies studied in this book, the only case in which exchanges of this type occur is that of Air Liquide. The other firms are either not vertically integrated (CFDP), or they do not exchange non-standardized services (GTIE), or they produce everything locally (Colas). This type of exchange belongs then with companies whose vertical upstream integration requires them to produce on a wider scale than that of the local unit.

The first type of exchange for Air Liquide is carried out between regions – units close to clients in the field – and national production establishments. For certain gases, these national establishments supply regions with full cylinders. The regions then send the cylinders back after using the contents. For the gases concerned, product flow is continuous between the production establishments and the regions. When a region receives an order, this information is automatically passed on to the corresponding establishment. The customer's order is delivered the following day by the region, which then takes back the empty cylinders. These cylinders are then exchanged for full ones the next day at the production establishment. The relationship between production establishments and the regions seems to be considered by most of the actors as a type of customer–supplier relationship. This relationship is moreover formalized by an agreement between each production establishment and each region, and transfer costs are applied to all the transactions between the two. However, these transfer costs are calculated centrally on a national scale. Cost negotiation is therefore not carried out directly between regions and production establishments. However, there are frequent contacts at the operational level between people responsible for distribution, which deal with adjustments of the flow. The perception about the nature of relations between the regions and the establishments are similar for both parties: 'The regions are our customers; there isn't any difference . yet, at the same time, if someone makes a totally stupid request, our response is different internally from that which we would make externally. If the request is impossible, we reply: 'you know very well that we cannot.' For more typical requests, everything is carried out as it would be with normal customers, we do everything we can . The relationships are autonomous and settled without calling upon management.' 'We avoid stirring up any disagreements . I never refuse, but there are sometimes delays.' 'We are suppliers. We try to respond to their demands, but because we function as just-in-time suppliers, we cannot make any mistakes . th ere are transfer prices, the regions are considered as customers. There is no invoicing, but we are committed by partnership contracts: relational aspects are important. The only thing that does not exist is the invoicing, but there is a system of transfer every month.' Under similar conditions, the production companies also take care of the maintenance, inspection, and replacement of cylinders.

The Transport Logistics Department (TLD) plays the same role as the national establishments in supplying regions with liquid gas (i.e. gas that is conserved and transported in large cryogenic reservoirs, and not in cylinders). Delivery is organized around five national centers which deliver directly to the regions and their customers. Customers are only in contact with the regions, but the trucks that deliver the liquid gas to them are those of the TLD. The regions also receive deliveries for their own needs. In spite of its name, the TLD does not play a managing role, and the relationship with the regions is of the same nature as that which exists with the production establishments.

The logic of the customer supplier relationship is not limited to supplying gas; it also applies to a considerable number of other peripheral units. These are technical support units or units which deliver equipment. If intervention in the region is not necessary, these units must supply the regions according to their needs, as happens with the supply of gas. A regional manager describes the simplicity of the relationship with these units: 'If we need to maintain a large cryogenic stock, it is bought centrally and made available to the region...we spend our time installing and dismantling the equipment at the customer's premises. The chances of re-employment are strong in the other regions; everything that is standard must be managed centrally and must always be available.' Some of these units are attached to the Industrial Department, but are not seen as having any real directive powers, as one account manager told us: 'We place an order for equipment or we call them about a technical problem. They act as consultants; I don't think of them as management.'

Exchanges within Air Liquide have two special characteristics. On the one hand, the regions do not have the option of procuring their supplies from outside the group. On the other hand, the basic transfer prices are centrally negotiated. Once the process has been started, there are still some adjustments which must be made during the operation. It follows that it is impossible for the central management to coordinate the many adjustments needed for the considerable number of deliveries. It is around the quality of service given by the supplying units (the delays, in particular, are crucial) that the adjustments between units are structured and not around prices. One of the essential points that emerges from interviews is the importance of the quality of the relationships between internal suppliers and regions. The true objective of the supplying unit must be to meet the regions' needs. For their part, the regions must clearly reveal the constraints under which they are working without requesting impossible feats of prowess. In many of the interviews, a real concern for reaching this balance, this spirit of cooperation between units, comes across. One possible alternative to an exclusive relationship is obviously the possibility of having recourse in some cases to external suppliers: this is the logic that is applied within GTIE for subcontracted projects between units. However, as will be shown when we deal with this issue in the section on links between market and network, this choice threatens the cooperative approach to the relationship between units.

The Management and Canvassing of Shared Customers

In all four of the case studies, units were able to share the same customers under certain circumstances. Two situations can arise: collaborative management of certain accounts and canvassing by the other units in the group.

The problem of collaborative management of certain accounts arises when units which have an exclusive geographic area are solicited by a customer for another area. The first question to resolve is which unit will do the job. For the three groups concerned (Air Liquide, Colas, and GTIE), the local unit is the one that is used. In certain cases the customer wants even so to have only one contact or only one invoice. This is particularly true of payments that can be relatively standardized, such as the supply of gas. At Air Liquide, the customer's account is managed by the initial region, and then compensation takes place between the regions. The same problems are found at GTIE and Colas for private customers. In general, solutions to these management problems are found directly between the units themselves, and recourse to arbitration by the center occurs only exceptionally. So, at Air Liquide, the regional managers 'are encouraged to resolve problems among themselves. If the situation comes up the line again, the regional managers are told to deal with it themselves, and they are made to understand that such behavior is not appreciated.' Within Colas, the geographical division, which follows the boundaries of the Departmental Directorate of Equipment (DDE), makes this kind of problem relatively rare, but the same logic of dialogue between agencies is found as a principle of management: 'the only case is that in which a private client from another agency chooses to establish himself in our sector: in this case, the other agency carries out the construction in consultation with us.'

However, canvassing represents a more sensitive point. At GTIE and CFDP in particular, there are possibilities of canvassing other units' customers. At GTIE, many companies are operating in closely associated sectors. It is therefore possible for one company to help other companies within the group to enter into contact with its own customers and so to enlarge the GTIE range supplied to a particular customer. In the case of CFDP, delegates who work for a company's agent can use that agent to help another delegate introduce himself to a different agent of the same company in another sector. The agents of a company that works with CFDP can therefore recommend the company for another area.

Yet, in this case as in the other, these possibilities are rarely or insufficiently exploited, and the difficulty of the approach is often emphasized. Thus, for certain GTIE actors, even if technical information is quite easily distributed among the companies in the group, commercial information remains less transparent. People hesitate to give away their contacts: 'It is easier to talk about the difficulties than to get people to give away information about their contacts. People are afraid that the other person in the group will not be up to it and that the customer will be lost.' 'In general, people give little information about their customers, everyone looks out for his own interests.'

Several explanations are given in both cases. First of all, there is a tendency to hold on to one's own clientele, a logic of private turf, that results from the way in which the units are involved in their local universe. Therefore, actors do not want spontaneously to reveal their contacts. The customers are at the heart of the area of autonomy given to agents, and they constitute a real key resource for the peripheral unit. A second explanation found in both GTIE and CFDP is the fear of losing customers. Even if there is no direct competition, one must have enough confidence in the competence of other units to recommend them to an important customer. There is therefore a fear of the other unit's failure: 'If I recommend my customer to another unit and that unit fails in the relationship, the loss of confidence can be very important to me.' Therefore actors may tend to avoid embarking on inter-unit cooperation of this type. This is even more true since the reciprocity of the exchange is not very clear, at least in the short term: if one unit allows another to contact one of its customers, it is not certain that any reciprocal contact will be possible or will happen. Certainly, if operations of this type multiply, compensation may come to a third unit; but the perceived risk often seems to exceed the hope of a counterpart. In this area, which is the reserved territory of the autonomous units, the group's interest does not seem to have priority. The center does not have any real means of intervention in this matter – if only by incentive – without calling into question one of the essential elements of its units' autonomy. The links and confidence that exist between individuals are therefore an essential element if they are to contemplate opening up their portfolios of clients to each other outside a partnership project.

COLLABORATIVE PROJECTS

Whether it be too small or whether it does not have the necessary skills at its disposal, there are requests that one unit cannot satisfy on its own. It is therefore possible for it to work with another unit from the group in co-contracting or subcontracting operations. These cases are no longer a question of simple transfers in which the need for direct coordination is in general rather limited. In fact, within a group, once an initial experiment has been carried out, the way to conduct standard transfers between units can easily be signposted. However, particular projects may require specific coordination and will necessarily be more difficult to standardize. Nonetheless, the implications of collaborative projects, both in the short and long term, are rather clear for the peripheral units involved: they concern carrying out concrete projects together, usually intended for a specific customer. The main limits to the development of this type of operation are to be found in the lost opportunities arising from poor knowledge of the network. Furthermore, the organization of projects between units requires moving beyond habits of compartmentalization and of isolation among units. It also entails good knowledge of the other unit and a certain open-mindedness. This internal cooperation can require a certain flexibility of structures, because the structures created as a result of collaboration can only be developed in the longer term if the units and the individuals can work in the harmonious manner which is necessary. Actors also insist upon the necessity of a clear division of roles, in the same way as they would for work with external units. Table 4.2 shows the main conclusions concerning collaborative projects between units.

Table 4.2 Collaborative projects

DIMENSION	OBJECTIVES	LIMITS
Collaborative Projects	• Responding to a request that exceeds the capacities of a unit	• Missed opportunities • Compartmentalization
Flexible structures	• Joint work on concept and realization	• Compatibility of individuals • Clear division of roles

Implementing Collaborative Projects

GTIE is certainly the case study in which projects between units are the most widespread. Such projects also exist at Air Liquide; certain support units have been created in order to work on collaborative projects with the regions. Finally, certain projects are found at CFDP and Colas between regions and diversified subsidiaries. In all these cases, collaborative work is built around a particular request that cannot be met by one single peripheral unit.

The simplest cases are those of large-scale projects that exceed the production capacity of a unit. Certain examples of this are found at GTIE and even at CFDP. At Colas, large projects are not always handled by the regions. This is done in order to avoid losing local customers in the interest of a project which is necessarily short-lived. Another peripheral unit takes care of this type of operation, one that is used for this sort of work: the Large Works Unit, whose operation is described in the following section.

The second case in which the cooperation of several units is required is that of projects which make use of multiple competences such that no unit by itself contains them all. At GTIE, where companies operate in complementary but distinct trades, these kinds of projects are frequent. Projects of the same nature, though very different in their practical implementation, are found at Air Liquide for projects that involve the regions on the one hand and the CEPIAs (Testing Centers) or particular support teams on the other. Projects of this nature exist as well between Colas' diversification subsidiaries (erection of roadsigns/signals, and equipment) and local agencies of the company's main activity (road building). In general, such projects are responses to calls for tender for both road resurfacing and the erection of roadsigns or security equipment. Such invitations to tender are rather rare. When the opportunity presents itself, the agencies always call upon the other companies of the group. There is no rule that imposes this, but as the subsidiaries are the leaders in their markets, it seems natural that the agency managers call upon the subsidiaries. The agency and the diversification subsidiary therefore work together on the project, and each plays its own part. In this case, the diversified subsidiaries do not compete with one another, but the bidding process is such that it is in the interest of each subsidiary to make the best bid it can. An agency manager says, for example: 'If business comes forward, we can make responses by mixing our competences: we sign on with them. [...] They are forced to bring down their prices because their proposal is integrated within the bid. [...] If I want to go through someone else, no one will say anything, I can. In my opinion, we go through them because they are the leaders. They are part of the group and they are the best.'

The same logic can be found at GTIE where the first objective of 'meshing' (running cross-cutting links between units) is a collaborative response to calls to tender for reasons of their size or because they require complementary competences. Management regards it as a strategic strength to be able to put together a cross-cutting bid: 'If we cannot do that, we do not advance, it is a standard practice. It can cut off business from competitors or, if we do not know how to do it, from ourselves. It is difficult to put a figure on cooperation because it does not appear directly in the company accounts.' Management makes its desires known in general terms, but the interaction between units is very open: there is no direct constraint on 'meshing' operations. Management does not intervene in the discussions between units, nor in the nature of collaborative operations. There is even a desire not to interfere, because intervention is seen as generating disruptions in the transaction. As a regional manager indicates: 'everything happens directly and, in order for it to go well, in general, it must happen directly between the companies. As a result, we maintain that the advantages and satisfactions linked to autonomy are superior to its problems. When hierarchy intervenes in matters concerning interdependencies, it only multiplies the problems.' Furthermore, the volume of transactions between companies is substantial, and, given the lightness of GTIE's central structures, they could not be coordinated directly by central management.

The realization of a collaborative project by two units does not necessarily involve a modification of structures. In the majority of cases, a subcontracting or co-contracting arrangement is sufficient. This is the solution most often used by GTIE. As a general rule, one of the companies decides to respond to an offer to tender and prefers to steer it within a subcontracting plan. Blockages can result from co-contracting arrangements, which seem more difficult to carry out: 'It poses a psychological problem, as the business managers prefer to have more elbow room. In periods of overload, co-contracting occurs more easily than in slow periods.' Under other circumstances, a collaborative response is envisaged in which the logic of co-contracting, where each unit takes care of one part of the services, comes into play.

However, launching such operations does not happen by itself. In the absence of any directive from the center, it is likely that such opportunities will be missed. If the units are to embark on this type of project, the individuals involved must know each other beforehand, and socialization must have already occurred. This is even more necessary because there is a temptation for units that have a very well delimited strategic project already not to break out of it, even if the mobilization of a wider bid will give them a strong competitive edge. Such limits can be found both at GTIE where 'meshing' is not imposed on units and at Air Liquide where the regions do not have the option of turning to companies outside of the group. In all of the cases, it is possible that a team will not be called in if the local actors are not able to identify the right contact person. As one manager points out, some opportunities for collaborative work can remain untapped: 'We don't always keep in mind the importance of disseminating the message that at GTIE we can do anything.' Aside from the identification of a contact person, the coordination of the operation does not require the intervention of the center. The problem that arises is the question of whether or not to cooperate, but in any case the units are perfectly capable of cooperating without the intervention of the central unit. Autonomous adjustment is once again the rule.

The Flexibility of Structures

For some operations, it is necessary to modify existing structures by creating cross-cutting project teams or even independent structures. This goes beyond the simple juxtaposition of activities in the framework of a project and the operation requires a certain flexibility on the part of the sub-units. This imperative arises in numerous cases where a significant amount of coordination and, in general, all the conceptual work must take place collaboratively.

This is the case for some of GTIE's electrical projects. The horizontal structure and the fact that there is only one hierarchical level within each company facilitate the formation of ad hoc teams for a particular project within the group. The structures are thus sufficiently flexible to allow a cross-cutting team which is capable of responding to a particular offer to be put in place rapidly. Then, 'after the operation, everyone returns to his or her place. The implementation can be very quick. When it comes to creating a new legal entity, there may be intervention by the regional manager, as this is a little more complicated.'

This schema is also found at Air Liquide, for example, for certain installations carried out on customers' premises: a joint team is set up for the period of assessment and installation, and then the region takes over for service and maintenance. This is particularly the case for Floxal, mini-factories that produce gas, which are set up directly on customers' premises. The logic of development is very different from that which corresponds to sales of gas in cylinders. One case is concerned with selling a product and the services that are associated with it, while in the other case Air Liquide makes an investment (the machine on the clients' premises remains the property of Air Liquide) and this investment must be made profitable by a long-term contract. The Floxal teams are mini-engineering units that put experts at the regions' disposal to carry out the assessment and implementation of this type of installation. A team for a given project would typically comprise: a sales manager and an account executive from the region, as well as a sales engineer and a technician from the Floxal team. The team is lead by Floxal sales engineers who operate in that region: 'The idea is the following: We are commissioned by the region. It is a partnership, and, when the project is completed, the region follows up the operation.' The Floxal team disappears after the installation: maintenance is completely decentralized, and members of the project team must be able to take over at that stage.

The example of the Large Works Unit at Colas also illustrates the need to systematically recombine structures. The Large Works Unit, which is perfectly adaptable, is in some way an institutionalization of flexibility of structures. This unit does not have its own equipment and it comprises only a construction manager, several construction engineers, a secretary, and a surveyor. The unit studies a certain number of cases and undertakes the work with the means already on site or with the help of the agencies that are geographically the closest. The revenues received by the Large Works Unit on agency's territory are then put back into the agency for the analytical evaluation of the agency's results. The creation of the unit corresponds to the desire not to disrupt local activity by non-renewable construction works. Because the Large Works Unit does not have its own resources, it is obliged to work by means of the agencies. This coordination does not seem to pose any particular problem: 'We assess the job together and it is the Construction

Manager from the Large Works Unit who monitors the progress of the works. We (or other agencies) supply the teams and the equipment. We then recover the whole profit margin.' However, conflicts of competence arise more often in the relationship between the Large Works Unit and the agencies than in the relationship between the agencies themselves. The Large Works Unit operates in the agencies' own geographic sectors, and it is not always easy to determine whether a construction project falls within the competence of the agency or within that of the Large Works Unit: 'There is always a bit of frustration when a project has been *snatched up* by the Large Works Unit... Head Office settles the problem when a conflict arises between a agency and the Large Works Unit on the subject of responding to invitations to tender or to lend equipment.'

Even though these examples deal with operations carried out within the same group, in all of the cases stress is laid on the need to specify the rules of the project very strictly. Because the project is actually handled internally, there is a natural tendency to be less exact, and this can be the origin of unanticipated behavior that is even more damaging because it comes from an actor from inside the group. The rules of the project must clearly establish the role of each team member, even in cases which do not involve external agents. Thus, at Air Liquide, in collaboration between the Floxal teams and the regions, it is important to specify who will lead the project during its conceptual and installation phases. It is also important to stipulate the distribution of costs or outcomes of the installation. So, in order to facilitate and clarify the transactions between the regions and the Floxal teams, accounting for the project in real terms has to be done, with the engineers' hours included in the investment. The manager we questioned emphasized the importance of the formalization of relationships before beginning a project: 'Formalizing all the steps is very important for motivation, efficiency and clarity in relationships. It allows the project to function smoothly.' The first experiments were more difficult at GTIE where the management of inter-company relations is more complex and less easily standardized: GTIE's activities are more diverse than those at Colas. Behavior tended to be more opportunistic, and in some cases tensions arose. In all the cases, the operation's success and its durability were both tied to the compatibility of the individuals who had to work together. If links are made between the project managers, it is quite possible that other projects for the same customer or for other customers will arise.

Whatever they may be, we have found examples of modification of structures in all the cases studied. These teams or ad hoc structures are more or less common, have a longer or shorter life, and mobilize (or do not mobilize) individuals for all of their time, but they are found repeatedly.

Furthermore, except for auxiliary issues (such as the creation of autonomous legal units by GTIE), this structure of cooperation is created systematically without the intervention of the center.

5. Towards a community of exchange

Transfer and collaborative projects are concrete operations; as well as these, peripheral units can work together on their knowledge and competences. They can pass on particular knowledge, making possible the diffusion of competences that have already been acquired by a unit, or they can work together within more or less formal groups to develop new competences. Beyond this rather ill-defined type of activity, peripheral units can be brought together to make decisions collaboratively that go beyond their usual sphere of action. Thus they enter the field of collegiate decision-making, which can lead to the formation of an emergent center. For this, a dialogue which is rich in content must be established, and this is not always easy. In the first two sections of this chapter we study to what extent the peripheral units are capable of involving themselves in collective activities, beyond their concerns of ongoing operational tasks. Existing compartmentalization, hierarchical reflexes, or even syndromes like that of 'not invented here' are similarly an impediment to putting into practice this community of exchange and collective decision-making.

Even though exchanges and collective decisions are difficult, peripheral units necessarily form an interconnected whole that can be called a community. There is a natural cohesion that emerges between these units, interconnected in their development and sharing internal suppliers; they share common interests and a form of cooperation cannot but be established between them. The coherence of their development is also influenced by their similarity of form and the bonds that they maintain with their local environment.

Sharing Knowledge and Building Competences

The point of departure for the selection of cases in this study was the existence of autonomy given to the peripheral units. This considerable autonomy, as well as tying the peripheral units into a network of local relationships, allows the development of local competences and the proposal of original solutions to problems that come up in the field. Autonomous peripheral units are confronted with two distinct problems. First of all, they run the risk of 'reinventing the wheel.' It often happens that problems that arise for one particular unit will have already found their solution in another unit. There are also cases in which one specialized unit can easily bring its knowledge to a unit that belongs to another area of expertise. The second problem is isolation. The existence of dialogue allows new knowledge to appear, leading to the development of new collective competences. Cross-cutting work between units, sometimes formalized, allows peripheral units to break out of the isolation created by autonomy. It is important to keep in mind that it is necessary not to try to systematize these types of contacts. They lose their purpose if they do not result directly from the desire of the peripheral actors. Table 5.1 shows the principal conclusions concerning the sharing of knowledge and elaboration of competences.

Table 5.1 Sharing competences

DIMENSION	OBJECTIVE	LIMITS
Informal Networks	• Mobilizing local knowledge	• Hierarchical boundaries • Compartmentalization • 'Not invented here'
Communities of practices	• Multi-unit exchanges	• Systematization • Loss of purpose • Poor information

Informal Networks

In all the cases studied, there are informal links between the units. Beyond the exchange of particular information, they can allow units, whether or not they are in the same business to transfer knowledge to each other.

If the units are in the same business, the idea is to arrange discussion between individuals who have been confronted with the same problems or situations. This can range from an open discussion over the telephone of a very simple problem between the people involved to going further and organizing an actual transfer of competences that can lead to setting up further formal mechanisms. The delegates at CFDP and the regions at Air Liquide practice this type of exchange extensively.

Within CFDP, the informal relationships between delegates are frequent, and there are no real barriers. If a delegate needs information or advice, or if he needs to be brought up to date on a project, all he needs to do is pick up the telephone. As they say themselves, the delegates are well informed on the experiments carried out in other regions: 'We exchange many faxes, telephone calls; for example, today I had eight telephone calls from delegates talking about practical aspects...ideas circulate rather well. If someone is interested in an idea, he can call the delegate directly.' 'Information often circulates by hearsay; then we have a meeting.'

The same freedom of exchange can be found between the regions of Air Liquide on a global scale. The appeal to a particular expertise can help a precise problem to be resolved or can lead to a real exchange of knowledge: 'There are isolated small businesses that do not have the chance to discuss things. We can make up for everything. We have access to a 'global village' via experts and cc-mail [the name of the internal email system]. For example, we set up an operation for the Formula One Grand Prix. Some Australians contacted us and asked us what we were selling to Formula One. They sold exactly the same thing for the Melbourne Grand Prix.' Emailing allows rapid communication between members of the group. The methods of coordination are varied and quite open.

The same principles can be found in cases where the peripheral units have particular specializations. This situation exists at Air Liquide. This specialization allows specific knowledge to be mobilized easily within the group. Such contacts are particularly abundant in the cases of Air Liquide and CFDP. Even at GTIE, where there are fewer exchanges, the possibilities are significant. The people interviewed indicate, for example for GTIE, that freedom of exchange and its possibilities are real: 'If we lack a certain technique, we can talk to specialists from these obscure areas. Access is very free and open. We can very easily call people within the group... as soon as there is a problem, I get in touch with my former colleagues to get the information.' 'If we need some expertise, we find it. We have the means, we can find competence on which we can draw'.

It is therefore clear that in all these cases, local knowledge or solutions have been developed, and some of these are transferable to other units. However, there are factors that limit the exchanges that are actually carried out.

The first limit to this type of relationship is the 'not invented here' syndrome. There is always the tendency to want to reinvent a solution thus facilitating appropriation. Solutions that come from outside a unit can be viewed as intrusions into the automonous territory of the peripheral actors. This type of behaviour was mentioned many times by people at Colas: 'It is difficult to spread from one agency to another. If ideas are passed on, it is done by the subsidiary. It isn't easy for them to communicate directly. Exchanges mainly concern roadworks and equipment. We even sometimes see the same experiments repeated elsewhere.' A similar logic can be found when certain CFDP delegates refuse the management help of other delegates, even if there is a real difference in competences between the sets of representatives. Some delegates pull back; they tend to feel attacked if another representative wants to help them in their work.

On the other hand, the smooth functioning of these informal exchanges at Air Liquide and CFDP can be explained by a desire to open up. In both cases, this is both a hierarchical and a horizontal opening-up. Informal relationships do not pose any problem at CFDP. At Air Liquide, it is widely known that everyone has the opportunity to deal directly with the person who has the knowledge, no matter what his hierarchical level or unit. However, the compartmentalization between units is more marked at Colas. Even if, as they state at Colas, 'there is no desire for compartmentalization (for example, each agency's budget is known.) compartmentalization exists in any case.' There are insufficient relations between agencies. I am sure that there are innovations elsewhere that we know nothing about.' Finally, at GTIE, the connections between units or with the center all go almost exclusively through the company managers.

Moreover, it is necessary to be able to identify the right person to speak to within the group. Even when compartmentalization is involuntary and arises from not knowing who is the appropriate person to contact, it can limit the possibilities of knowledge exchange, including groups within which informal exchanges work well. Thus, at Air Liquide: 'The system of relationships is delicate. Certain units should move closer to other Air Liquide entities and do not do so. They do not know who are the right people who can solve the problem. it is very important to choose the right contact person in each unit.'

The actors of the periphery also emphasize the importance of relations between individuals in ensuring real, in-depth exchanges. The human aspects, the knowledge of one another, are therefore essential: 'It happens through human beings. You have to know each other to get to this level. Otherwise, it is difficult. We do not have the reflex sufficiently to go and find out each other's competences: we contact the people we know'; 'It is necessary that people know each other: they have to know what the others can do. This becomes increasingly difficult as the group grows.' We will come back to the opportunities for meeting together which are created by the center of the group; these play an essential part in getting people to know each other.

Communities of Practices and Other Groups

More systematic links can be set up between the peripheral units in order to exchange ideas on more or less precise points. Whether they are called networks and clubs, as at Air Liquide, clubs as at GTIE, or even groups, as at CFDP, these recurrent meetings encourage open exchange between peripheral units. Most of them are close to the definition of communities of practices if we acknowledge that communities of practices can be managed to a certain degree or grown by a sustaining activity from the central management. Air Liquide, GTIE, and CFDP offer good examples of the possibilities and limits of attempts to encourage the development of communities of practices while trying not to kill their spontaneity, a very difficult exercise indeed.

At CFDP several groups have been set up successively around particular themes. These groups can be formed independently or according to a particular need expressed by the Inter-Regional Committee (the central collegial structure). In all cases, there is no restriction on their questioning the organization or actual practices, a complete freedom of speech. The example of the 'Lille group' at CFDP shows clearly how far the company is ready to go in order to encourage open exchanges between delegates. Throughout 1996, the delegates met in Lille in order to hold discussions in parallel with the Inter-Regional Committee. The declared theme was to bring their thoughts to a discussion about the development of the company. The composition of this group in parallel with the usual structure of representation soon caused it to be viewed as 'a dissident group which only brought together delegates who were against the current plan.' Some delegates spoke of a putsch, when members of the Lille group asked the owners of the firm to carry their reasoning through to its logical conclusion and to withdraw completely from the decision-making process so that the delegates could take ownership of the structures. What is interesting about this phenomenon, which remained relatively limited in its effects and in its duration, is the reaction of the other delegates. It is not within the logic of CFDP either to forbid or exert pressure. The Lille group therefore continued to meet for a while before disbanding completely as the plan advanced. Even those who emphasized the aspects which might have been disturbing about this group indicated in this connection that 'dialogue is important and members of the group needed to speak to each other.'

At Air Liquide 'networks' are set up in order to encourage the emergence and the sharing of knowledge and competences. Networks constitute a flexible mode of coordination between the people in the company who want to share their knowledge and who have common problems or concerns. The idea is to link people who are alone in their region. Networks meet together every three or four months for one or one and a half days. There is a guarantor elected from among the members of the network. In theory, anyone can set up a network; one must speak about it with one's director beforehand. All the same, the need must be justified, and so there aren't any networks for operators, drivers, etc. Certain sales representatives regret not being able to exchange information with their colleagues from other regions: 'There is not a sales rep network, and we have less and less to do with other regions...

training sessions allow discussions within the trade. We regret not having the opportunity to see what happens elsewhere.' On the other hand, there are managers who belong to several networks, like the regional managers of customer relations or regional directors: 'There is a network of regional managers that brings together seven regions and meets every six weeks. Another network of four regions meets on our initiative. These networks exchange ideas, solve common problems... We could stay outside the network, but we would lose a lot.' The make-up of the networks is very open, and the results seem very encouraging overall, at least for inter-regional relations. For an expert in information systems, 'some people are much stronger in computing and information technologies, others are better at dialogue and know better how to make sure that people learn to use a software. So we have exchanges, transfers of competences.' In the same spirit, a development manager says, 'the network is very open. It allows us to avoid feeling lost and is held together by affinity... we have to avoid having burdensome meetings; we have to talk about our difficulties. It works. We find a subject that interests everyone. We try, outside the meetings, to visit an interesting establishment. Meetings take place twice a year and last a day and a half. Meeting too often is useless.'

As for the clubs, they form a means of 'meshing' that is made available to the 'companies' of the GTIE group. The clubs operate on a quite informal level. They bring together a number of company managers, engineers and/or directors to reflect on a theme (there is not necessarily any chair). However, the creation of a club is generally a decision taken by the strategic orientation committee (thus, a central structure) usually on the basis of a proposal from one or several directors or company managers. Although limited to certain actors (company managers and engineers), the clubs make real collaborative work possible. There are about forty of these clubs concerned with various themes. They can group together companies that have a common customer, that work in the same sector, or that want to develop a more specific theme (for example, there is a logistics club). The activity can be temporary or it can become permanent. Clubs distribute minutes to participants and possibly a report at the end of their activity. They are essentially viewed as tools that allow contacts to be established within the group. As certain people point out: 'the clubs and discussion groups allow people to get to know other people and their activities; so asking for information becomes easier.' 'The purpose is to exchange contacts, as well as difficulties encountered.'

We are talking about groups whose impact is relatively limited. They do not make decisions that concern the entire company, but rather bring together people who have common concerns. In fact, two types of groups can be distinguished. The first type has a relatively precise purpose, for example, users of a particular tool or units that operate in a particular domain. A second type of group, represented by the networks of Air Liquide, is made up of individuals who carry out the same functions within different sub-units and thus are closer to communities of practices. In both cases, the objective is to allow individuals who belong to autonomous structures and who are therefore relatively isolated within these structures to share their knowledge and possibly deal with their problems together. This type of group allows for the introduction of a way of thinking that can be described as multi-local (it does not concern the entire company, but rather a certain number of its sub-units) while avoiding using hierarchical centralization to handle the problem.

One of the lessons that can be drawn from Air Liquide's success in this area, from certain vexations at CFDP and certain reservations expressed by GTIE, is quite certainly the risk incurred by this type of group if it is too formalized or systematized. This is the very core of the question of how manageable communities of practices can be. Firstly, these groups must remain sufficiently unconstrained to stay creative, and, secondly, they must not have systematization imposed upon them. The relative failures of some groups at CFDP are very striking in this respect: not all the delegates wanted to meet to discuss general themes at the same time. The systematization of 'universities' – discussion groups with a general remit – has thus been poorly viewed: 'We always find the same problem at CFDP: when an attempt is made, we try to systematize it, and it doesn't work. We have not found an objective for such universities.' The risk associated with generalization is the loss of the group's purpose, which leads to a decrease in motivation. People must thus be allowed to meet, but it seems useless to impose this type of meeting on the units, if they do not feel the need to share and develop knowledge. In contrast, smooth functioning of this type of group is based, on the one hand, on the identification of themes that can serve as the focus for the group and, on the other hand, on the existing links between individuals who can decide to meet independently of a specific subject to consider (this is the case of the 'networks' at Air Liquide).

COLLEGIAL DECISION-MAKING

In some cases, peripheral units can come to make joint decisions that go beyond the field of intervention of one particular unit. Such cases fall more or less clearly into the domain of collegiality: the peripheral units partially decide for the whole organization or at least for a part of the organization. They can concern relatively limited participation in the frameworks of working groups or local coordination between units. The case of CFDP shows us that it is possible to go much further, but it also illustrates the difficulty of the approach. Collegiality, if it concerns a project which goes beyond simple economic considerations, can lead to considerable difficulties. If the project is completely implemented, there is the risk that decision-making will be slowed down and that motivation will decrease. The other pitfall is that of a collegiality that is truncated by hierarchical intervention or by the appearance of conflicts between units. Table 5.2 shows the main conclusions concerning collegial decision-making.

Table 5.2 Collegial decision-making

DIMENSION	OBJECTIVES	LIMITS
Working group	• Including local actors in the decision	• Lack of decision • Hierarchical control
Management of resources	• Management of multi-local resources	• Conflict between units
Collegiality	• Helps ownership of the decisions	• Demotivation or disinterest • Slowing down of decision-making

Working Groups

A first step towards collegiality is taken when the center wants to consult the agents in peripheral units about certain decisions. This consultation can consist of dialogues during informal contacts between central and peripheral actors, but the approach can be made more systematic, with the center trying to include the periphery when important decisions are made. The working group is without doubt the only tool which exists in the four firms that more or less approaches a form of collegiality. The idea that serves as the foundation for the working groups that interest us here is the need to bring people from the field, holders of local knowledge, into the decision-making process. In some cases, working groups include people from the center (this happens regularly at Colas), but this need not be systematic (Air Liquide, CFDP, and GTIE). The general rule is always that the center starts by assigning a particular role to the group concerned. Without necessarily creating a formal working group, there are central meetings in all the four companies during which ideas can be tested and exchanges carried out directly between the units, but under the influence of the center.

These mechanisms, central meetings, and working groups are found in all the companies and more examples without much originality could be given. The situation as described by the actors at Air Liquide summarizes the situation well. If we take as an example the industrial department – a department marked by a hierarchy that is more important than that which can be seen in relations between the center and the regions – we find different opportunities for exchange between departmental management and the production establishment or the regions. First of all, there are some meetings. An engineer within one of the establishments points out: 'I attend two kinds of meetings, meetings between regional engineers and the Mixal follow-up group. These two meetings are essential. The organizer of the meeting, a person from the industrial department, sets the order of the agenda. We can add items to it. This allows us to channel the meeting; otherwise, we would talk about nothing. We are not mature enough to do it ourselves, and new subjects would not be brought up: the experts can bring a lot [to these meetings]. This leads us to build links between ourselves. The meetings also give direction to where we go; one mustn't confuse autonomy with lack of guidance.' Meetings are thus viewed as an important part of the group's cohesion; meetings also reassure the people present. There is also the desire to disseminate innovations and suggestions that can come up within establishments: 'When initiatives come from the field, we validate the ideas, possibly by testing them, and we pass them on to other establishments or even on to regions or globally.' Beyond the consolidation of field initiatives, people want to question adopted decisions. Thus, regarding procedures, a member of the industrial direction points out: 'When we introduce a procedure, we ask: "Do you agree? Will you apply it?" There are people who make up their own procedures.' Associating actors from the field with decision-making also happens by setting up working groups at all levels. Unlike networks, which are formed freely among members of the company, working groups are created through the initiative of the center and have a much more precise goal: 'The project is entrusted to us by general management. The person who manages the group chooses who will be in it. There can be mini working groups in the regions.' The working group is therefore not necessarily run by someone from the department. There are also groups based on precise themes that are similar to the meetings organized by management.

Without entering completely into the field of collegiality, that is to say, towards collective decision-making, management meetings and working groups allow collaborative reflection between peripheral actors and those from the center. This reflection nourishes the decision-making process.

However, these types of meetings or groups do not generally constitute a decision-making body; they are rather examples of consultation, while the decision is taken centrally. Moreover, the openness of exchanges in a meeting or working group is clearly less than when actors meet in 'clubs' or 'networks.' This type of structure is necessarily constrained by the presence of people from central management.

Management of Multi-local Resources

A first step towards collegiality is the management of resources or of constraints that concern several peripheral units. Sharing resources is often at the origin of the creation of networks between independent companies. Conversely, there are very few examples at the internal level. When resources are shared between several units, we have found two solutions in the cases studied. The first solution is to entrust the management of the resources in question to a peripheral unit which becomes an internal supplier. This is the solution that was adopted in a large number of cases at Air Liquide. Its operation was described above. Another possibility is obviously to centralize the management of common resources. It does indeed seem simpler to entrust the management of the resources in question to a distinct functional unit which reports directly to the center of the group. This choice does not seem to pose any particular problem to the extent that the need to concentrate the activity concerned is justified in the eyes of all. Thus we can explain easily why we do not find collegial management of resources that are used by all sub-units. It is moreover one of the benefits of belonging to a large group.

On the other hand, there are cases in which particular needs affect several units, but not the entire group. These may concern the management of resources which can be described as multi-local, that is to say shared by several units with closely related specialties or geographical proximity. In such precise cases, it seems easier to resort to autonomous adjustments between units. Good examples of this type of decision can be found in the case of Air Liquide. At Air Liquide, the managers of neighboring regions have to coordinate their actions in order to tie themselves into arrangements to handle emergency interventions, to coordinate the resort to multi-regional development experts, and to optimize deliveries to neighboring regions. The relationship with multi-regional development experts is handled in effect by the salespeople who contact them directly to deal with a particular problem. As the regional managers pointed out, the relationship is a work relationship that does not pose any particular problem: 'The work is always done on fixed dates and days, except for urgent needs. In general, there is no problem. The development experts have good professional awareness. They are there when we need them, and we do not take advantage of them.'

The regional managers are thus led to make joint decisions which concern several regions in some relatively limited specific domains. It is clear that these relations are restricted in range and that they remain manageable through direct links between the regions. It can be done in this specific case because of the quality of the relationship between the regions: the absence of competition and the truly cooperative context favors a non-conflictual management of resources.

Collegiality

The majority of companies stop at these embryonic manifestations of collegiality and do not go as far as to incorporate truly collective decision-making. The case of CFDP is an experiment in this domain, a model of what could be feasible in a company of greater size. In the other groups, we did not find any mode of operation that came close to that of CFDP. In these other cases, a method of sharing decisions may exist, but it always remains very limited. Yet it seems that it may be possible to transpose this dimension of the network mode of organization to some of the decisions made within large companies. The case of CFDP encourages both prudence and enthusiasm for the possibilities offered by collegiality.

Prudence first of all: if one thinks of the difficulties that the company encountered in finding a mode of organization that truly allowed it to make decisions in a collegiate manner. A quick summary of close to twenty years of research to find a suitable collegial form allows one to see clearly the difficulty of the approach. Four key steps mark the development of CFDP:

1. The creation of a system of delegation in 1982
2. The suppression of all hierarchical structures in 1990
3. The setting up of a collegial decision-making body in 1992
4. The inclusion of insurance intermediaries within the decision-making bodies in 1993

Throughout the 1970s, the number of CFDP's customers increased rapidly, and in 1982 the first system of delegation was created. The representative was responsible for the development of the company's activity in a given geographic area. From the start, a substantial degree of autonomy was given to the delegates. To coordinate their activity, a structure by area was implemented. The two area managers provided coordination and evaluation of the system of delegated management. With the multiplication of delegations, coordination by the area managers became increasingly difficult. It was also during this time that the company's two directors came to see more clearly what they wanted: they proposed a new mode of management. Their choice is shown as 'the elimination of all references to a statutory hierarchy.'

Hierarchical structure by area was therefore abolished. Regional coordinators were put in place in 1989. They carried out the job of delegate and were chosen for their experience and for the amount of time they had spent in the company. They were in charge of what went on in the region (four or five delegations). However, the regional coordinators quickly formed an intermediary hierarchical level that was judged undesirable. The system of regional coordinators was therefore abolished. In 1991 a structure of teams and 'functional facilitators' replaced it. All the delegates became facilitators in a particular domain for their team. The idea was to achieve a transfer of knowledge in this way. The system was however cumbersome to manage, and participation in its meetings became increasingly passive.

In the middle of 1992, the system of facilitators was definitively abandoned. A first collegial structure, the Service Coordination Structure, was created in 1992; this structure, following the announcement by the directors of their desire to leave the company in the medium term, was supposed to allow for a transfer of managerial competency to the delegates. The fifteen regional teams (there were now 60 delegations) were kept, and the SCS was made up of one representative from each of the fifteen regions (they were subsequently joined by the two company directors).

As the structure of the SCS did not achieve a consensual functioning and proved to slow down decision-making, a new structure was set up. Formal elections by secret ballot were organized at the end of 1993 in order to choose a group of five delegates, the G5. The G5 was intended to take charge of the factors that affected the whole company and to coordinate some discussions within the teams. The G5's first thoughts were to integrate the insurance intermediaries (clients of the company) very quickly into its deliberations. It therefore turned quickly into the G10, then into the G12, as the company directors' presence seemed necessary. This marked the beginning of a metamorphosis of the whole structure, in which the intermediaries played an important role. After about one year, the group produced its thoughts on the company's development and emphasized two principles: an organization that involved both the delegates and the insurance intermediaries, as well as a buyout of the company directors' shares by the representatives and the intermediaries.

Following the work of the G12, a new structure was gradually implemented by 1995, a structure that was based on bigger teams made up of two or three delegates and two or three intermediaries. The basic unit was no longer the delegation, but rather the twinned pairs of delegates and intermediaries. Because the G12 represented only five teams out of a total of fifteen, a second group was elected in February 1995, the G30. It was made up of fifteen twinned pairs with each pair representing a national team. The G30 therefore played a legislative role within the organization. It took a number of decisions which were implemented by the G10. The G30 also works by means of commissions on various themes. However, the division of powers between the G10 and the G30 quickly proved difficult. Tensions arose between the two groups and, as was the case for the SCS, the large number of people who were present in the G30 was damaging the efficiency of the group.

The current structure was put in place in 1996. It allows both the representation of all the teams, with movement towards collective decision-making and the transmission of information between the teams. A supplementary structural level was introduced: certain teams were changed, and the new teams were regrouped into six regions. The teams appointed a twinned pair of members (delegate and intermediary) to the regional committee; each region was then represented on the Inter-Regional Committee (IRC) which therefore is made up of twelve people. The company directors were allowed to attend the Inter-Regional Committee's meetings, but they did not necessarily do so: they are not part of the group. On the other hand, a Committee of Ethics and Orientation (CEO) has also been created, which is made up of two former directors and some former members of the Inter-Regional Committee.

The team structure, regional committee structure and inter-regional committee structure considerably improved the circulation of information within CFDP. Thanks to these structures, ideas spread: 'It is difficult to know where a project originates or the method of its transmission. But information circulates: I proposed an idea to the IRC in February, and seven days later, everyone knew about it.' The IRC is elected for a year and membership is non-renewable; the purpose of this is to avoid the appropriation of power as well as to ensure that a large number of delegates get to serve as members of the IRC. The idea is thus to encourage rapid understanding of the group's problems.

A more or less thorough consultation of the delegations and a lot of toing and froing can happen, depending on the importance of the decision being made: 'In cases in which it is urgent to come to a decision, the IRC decides. However, if more time is available, it is possible to go back and forth between the twinned pairs.' In general, no one can force a decision to be made. However, the IRC's legitimacy is based on election or designation of delegates by teams; its views thus come from the delegates and it can make decisions in their name. As one of the members of the IRC states, 'in the functional operation, nobody has any hierarchical power, but...as for the delegate, you are the representative, the member of the IRC. What you might say is therefore interpreted as a word of command... In fact, this makes the operation much stronger: we do not give any orders but what comes from the

IRC emanates from you and is discussed with you. A consensus emerges and therefore what is said is necessarily accepted.'

The lack of motivation or the disinterest of delegates is certainly one of the main problems posed by collegial decision-making. Indeed, the reactions of operationals seemed divided when they were initially asked to take part in and then to take charge of decisions that concerned the entire company. What then emerged was a certain lack of interest, because of the complexity of the structures put in place and the resultant slow pace of decision-making. This is undoubtedly an important lesson to be learned from groups like the SCS or the G30 which included too many individuals. The current structure, the result of this long process of learning, seems to be balanced. It allows for efficient and consensual decision-making. This experience shows that a collegial structure can obtain wide consensus within a company: the group of individuals placed at the center of the organization does not have the power of command, but decisions are viewed as legitimate because of the simple fact that they come from the entire company. The case of CFDP clearly shows that the majority of traditional companies fall far short of the possibilities offered by relations between peripheral units.

THE COMMUNITY OF PERIPHERAL UNITS

The peripheral units of a company generally find themselves in a position where they are bound together, well beyond the direct interventions of central management. They are interdependent first and foremost in terms of the supply that they represent collectively. Together they cover a competitive field that goes well beyond their own areas; in the framework of this wider field, they are jointly responsible for an image which is the image of the entire group; finally, outside any directive, they share common internal suppliers. Beyond this emergent cohesion arising at the periphery, the units have a similarity of form – they are often of small size and endowed with similar structures – and are involved in their local environment, even to the point of being under the control of this environment (this control is essentially exercised by the customers). This similarity of form, around a local plan, is particularly important where the coherence of the company's development is concerned. At this point we leave our principal concern, that of cohesion, and enter into the related area of coherence. That being said, this phenomenon is directly related to the autonomy of the peripheral units. We make the transition from cohesion between units to coherence of development which arises from the connections with external actors – in the majority of cases, the customer. Table 5.3 shows the principal conclusions concerning the foundations of this cohesion. This section is more the result of a conceptual construction carried out from observations made in the field than the result of consolidation of the observation of structures by the agents. This explains why the reader will not find quotations from interviews here, unlike the other sections of this chapter and the preceding one.

Table 5.3 The community of peripheral units

DIMENSION	OBJECTIVE	LIMITS
Emergent cohesion	• Playing on the effect of reputation • Concentration of certain resources	• Break-up • Free-riders
Similarity of form	• Local Adaptation • Cross-cutting points of reference	• Differentiation of units

An Emergent Cohesion

The peripheral units as a whole occupy a competitive field which, in the cases studied here, represents homogenous supply to the market. They occupy this competitive field collectively. They may comprise a group of closely related activities that belong to the same trade or they may exercise the same activity in different geographic zones. In this situation the trade imposes itself on the units, beyond the plan formulated by the central management. This mode of organization in distinct, but united units corresponds to the need for flexible development that is adapted to local constraints but that does not exclude the possibilities of sharing between units. The peripheral actors are perfectly aware of the fact that they make up a community, a group of units that provides homogenous global supply in the exercise of a trade which is the trade of the group. We find this idea of community constructed around a trade in all the four cases studied. It is clear that network organization cannot exist outside an industrial logic. The dimension of trade is undoubtedly a fundamental dimension that underlies every possibility of network cohesion. Thus the limit of cohesion by the network is reached here; it is set by the limit of the trade. In order for the network mode of organization to function, the competitive field in which the units are found must be sufficiently homogenous to be viewed as the reflection of a logic of trade. GTIE positions itself at the very limit of this logic, and the peripheral actors sometimes get bogged down in activities that can be seen as too heterogeneous to allow for collaborative work or to allow the network to function. This is without a doubt a limit to the network as a mode of organization: the risk of break-up arising from the failure to perceive the pertinence of supply that is too broad and too complicated.

Within a reasonably homogenous trade, everyone is responsible on a local level for the development of the group. Each unit is the representative of the group in a particular competitive field, whether it be a business or a geographic zone. The construction of the group's general image depends on the activity of each of the peripheral actors. The fact of belonging to a company that promotes a particular image is an asset only when each unit acts in accordance with the image held by external actors. A group has a good image and a strong reputation only insofar as local actions develop that image and that reputation. In industries such as those which we have studied, the effects of reputation play an important part and doubt can quickly set in if one of the peripheral units does not meet the clients' expectations. It is clear that the center can play an important regulatory role in such matters, but the units find their interest in a contribution that, consequently, they should make spontaneously. It is always attractive to act as free-riders: the effect of reputation works in both ways, and a peripheral unit can decide to live off the image developed jointly by the other units. This type of behavior was described by actors within CFDP. Certain delegates built up their clientele of insurance intermediaries, without adopting the partnership approach advocated by the collectivity of representatives. A delegation can live off the effect of reputation in this way for several years, but the company's competitive advantage in the medium term rests uniquely on the partnership that delegates are capable of establishing with the insurance intermediaries. Such free-riding behavior poses a serious risk to the entire company. The risk is even greater because reaction time can be rather long. A project of buyout by the delegates and insurance intermediaries that is currently in progress has, among other advantages, that of eliminating this type of behavior a priori: it is unlikely that a representative would participate in the buyout of a company if he did not believe in the project.

Peripheral units also share a certain number of internal suppliers, which helps to reinforce their cohesion. The center's role in this matter is not neutral. Certain central units have a power of command, and their interventions seem more like orders than advice. However, the center can also be freely solicited by the peripheral units as an internal supplier of advice. This attitude is found particularly often within Air Liquide and Colas. In these companies, the members of the central units are viewed as experts: in general, they come from the field and so have substantial experience that they can make available to the periphery. On any number of themes, the peripheral units are not required to approach them nor to take account of their advice, but they do it just the same, outside any hierarchical approach. A similar phenomenon appears with the recourse to peripheral units that are internal suppliers. This can be found at GTIE and Air Liquide. In the latter case in particular, the fact that it is obligatory to resort to internal suppliers is certainly not neutral. In GTIE's case, where a market relationship superimposes itself on the network organization, the convergence associated with the recourse to internal suppliers is less marked. The existence of internal service providers is connected with the need to make intensive use of certain resources. Apart from any constraint on supply, cohesion linked to recourse to internal suppliers works only when the quality of service is sufficient.

Similarity of Form

In all the cases studied, the peripheral units from the same group have similar forms. These units are centered around a local project which lies at the heart of their development. Because of the similarity of their form, they have common concerns. The strong similarity between units can serve as the basis for cross-cutting work. This similarity is once again the result of the constraint imposed by the division of the trade into a series of basic activities fulfilled by each of the sub-units. Each one has an objective and a different development plan, and yet they are very close because of their size, because of the similarity of the projects assigned to them and because of the structures with which they are endowed. One of the elements that facilitates setting up cross-cutting networks within Air Liquide is clearly this similarity in form. Once an issue that is likely to interest a certain number of individuals within the group has been identified, it is relatively easy to find guideposts within the structure and to identify those who would like to be involved. In the same way, the search for a particular form of expertise is greatly facilitated by the replication of structures at the international level. Whatever the country in which a person carries out his or her functions, the definition of his or her tasks is similar. It is therefore much easier to work together and to mobilize areas of expertise.

It is clear that local specificity makes a difference between different units of the same group, and it is in these differences that we should seek the limits of the factors making for cohesion. Thus, the similarity of forms plays a greater or lesser part in each of the cases studied, and within each case because of the nature of the units studied. GTIE is undoubtedly the case in which there coexist units that differ the most in their form and in their projects. Yet the similarity is strong between such autonomous units as are centered on a project that fits into the overall trade mission of the group. A certain number of benchmarks are always found in these situations: the importance of the managing director of each 'company' or the part played by account executives and project managers. Here again it is very easy for each person to imagine what he/she can expect of the others and to find his/here way around the operation of a unit with which he/she never even had contact.

6. The role of the center

The reader is now very familiar with the issues concerning the network organization, having mastered both its subtleties and limits. The presentation of the conclusions about the network gives a good idea of what peripheral units can do by way of mutual adjustment. But whatever the scope of mutual adjustments may be, is it possible to do completely without a body placed at the center of the network? The real question is how better to understand the role that a central body can play in the network organization. This center can take the form of traditional general management or can be an emergent center, as is the case at CFDP; in any case, the center can do much to support the network organization. The case of CFDP shows that, even if it is emergent, there is always the need for a central coordination unit. It is the role of this central unit which we seek to define here: how does it make it possible for the network to function? Three important roles of the center are significant for the development of the network organization. The center can first of all clarify the relationships between the peripheral units by defining the rules of these relationships. It then plays an essential role in creating and maintaining the dynamics of the network. Finally, it retains a certain number of fields where it must intervene.

DEFINING THE RULES OF THE GAME

Remember first of all that the center is at the origin of the initial project that underpins the constitution of a complex organization, which can become a network organization or not. It is on the basis of this initial project that the company as a whole is made up, center and periphery together. The evolution is thus very different from that which can be imagined when independent companies are regrouped into an external network. The periphery results from the project, and the structure in peripheral units results from the break-up of an original nuclear structure. It is clear that the evolution of the organization can lead, as in the case of CFDP, to the disappearance of the initial center in order to make way for an emergent core. In any event, the organization needs this core in order to continue its evolution. This center must in addition preserve its capacity to define and maintain the nature of the peripheral units and their activities. It must also be able to define the basic rules which govern the relations between the units themselves, as well as the terms of those relations.

Defining the Boundaries of Peripheral Units

It is up to the center to define the periphery's nature: what are the peripheral units and what do they do? The center is the guarantor of the coherence of choices carried out at this level. Indeed, these choices require an overall vision that cannot leave one peripheral unit isolated. The first element is the project of each peripheral unit. This project actually corresponds to the definition of the competitive field in which the peripheral unit will intervene: a particular activity or an activity in a particular geographic area.

The coherence of the projects is significant in two respects. Firstly, the juxtaposition of the projects must make it possible to cover the entire competitive field targeted by the group. Secondly, we have already pointed out the harmful effects of competition between peripheral units on the network organization. The projects must therefore be adjusted so that the entire competitive field is covered and there is no overlap that generates competition. This concept includes the geographic area, the customers who are envisaged and the competences which have been mastered.

GTIE uses criteria of this type to define the plans of the companies that make up the group. The positioning of each company is done according to three axes that correspond to the business that takes place. A geographic area can be associated with this business. The first axis is that of know-how: it concerns the type of service carried out, which is classified according to the pyramid of the 'Integrated Computer Manufacturer.' The know-how that is implemented ranges from simple competences directly related to machines to the management of computer-assisted production, including workshop management. The second axis is that of customers' practices and their field of activity (chemistry, cars, etc.). The third axis corresponds to the nature of the customers and the corresponding commercial competences. This can concern public or private customers and requires the ability to respond to invitations to tender or to work in partnership. The center can exert pressure that is more or less strong on the definition of the project, with an approach that is more or less bureaucratic, but its minimal role in the smooth operation of the network organization is to ensure the coherence of the projects which have been defined.

A second significant element is the internal structure with which the peripheral units are endowed. The network organization must be able to rely on an internal structure that is sufficiently open, on all levels, towards both the interior and exterior of the group. This opening is antithetical to an approach that is too strongly hierarchical in the internal relations of a peripheral unit. However, even at Air Liquide, the temptation is strong for the head of an autonomous unit to adopt a hierarchical mode of operation within his span of control. In some regions, the adaptation was difficult, and for a while, autonomy stopped at the level of the regional director: 'Some regional managers set up mini-hierarchies. You have to be wary. Other managers choose to decide everything.' The center must be able to protect the organization from such deviations if network cohesion is to be established. In addition, sharing a similar internal organization considerably helps contacts and relations between units (Air Liquide's networks are a good example). Furthermore, in all the cases studied it seems that the center plays a significant role in the definition of the internal structure of the units.

Defining the Rules of Interaction

The network organization emerges from the interactions between peripheral units, but this emergence does not simply happen. It needs to be guided and structured. The center has a significant role to play in the definition of the rules of the game: it can fix the conditions of the relationships and interactions between the units.

A first significant element is the way in which transfers and collaborative projects are organized, which leads to financial compensation between units. Here two possibilities can be recognized, that of Air Liquide, which is based more on an endogenous frame of reference, and that of GTIE, which relates itself more readily to the market. We have already discussed the possible margin of maneuver and the equilibrium to be found between reference to the market, needed if supply is to be undertaken, and excessive competition between joint contractors, subcontractors or internal suppliers, which puts the cooperative approach of the relationship into danger. No matter what choice is made – one can even suppose that several solutions coexist – the way in which relationships are conceived must be defined *ex ante* in order to avoid perpetual negotiations between units in a debate that could only be fruitless. One should not lose sight of the fact that everyone is in the same group and that any time spent on negotiating the distribution of the fruits of an operation between two units is a dead loss for the group as a whole. If balanced mechanisms are retained, it is certainly possible to avoid opportunistic behavior and transaction costs for which there is no place in the network organization.

The center can also play an essential role in defining a framework for the network organization. The peripheral actors need reference points and occasions when they can meet. It is clear that without discouraging the informal interactions that are so necessary, it is possible to create more formal occasions at which peripheral agents can exchange, work, reflect together, and meet each other. One finds here a whole range of tools, from meetings regularly organized by the center to the 'networks' proposed by Air Liquide to GTIE's 'working groups' or clubs. Some training activities can also be an opportunity to meet others and to discover common concerns, interests, customers, and problems. It is up to the central unit to define these formal occasions for meeting and socialization.

THE ENGINE OF THE DYNAMICS OF THE NETWORK

Even when the necessary structures have been created, it does not necessarily follow that the process will take off and that the network organization will take shape. The central unit can create the dynamic, prime the pump for relationships between peripheral units, which then develop autonomously. The first step is that of 'setting up the network': the center encourages meetings, finds the right contact people, and draws out common concerns. The second step is that of the use of clan organization to support the network.

Setting up the Network

Whatever the extent of its role, the central unit necessarily occupies a privileged position within the organization. The simple fact that the center works with all of the units on defining strategic plans gives it knowledge of the group as a whole, knowledge which the peripheral agents do not have at their disposal. Thanks to this privileged information, the central actors can selectively create connections between the units better than the others can. They can circulate basic information on competences and the work carried out by various units or put units that have common concerns in contact with each other. It is therefore essential that the center simply play the role of catalyst and that it does not manage the interactions between units directly. The regional managers at GTIE perfectly fulfill this role. They are content to point out possible operations and then let the peripheral units manage their relationships autonomously. Concern to act in this way is also found at Colas where the center's role is even more significant because the peripheral units have few direct contacts. This is even truer if an innovation or know-how can be diffused on the national scale: the transposition is usually made through the medium of the network and then from company headquarters. In the transfer of knowledge, the center does not command, but it can inquire about the work carried out in an agency or put peripheral actors who have common problems or concerns in contact with each other: For example, an agency had prepared a safety evaluation form for visits to building sites. This subsidiary took charge of it and circulated the form. Another agency chose to redefine the blank form before using it. For us there was no question of saying, 'From now on, you will fill out this kind of form.' It was related to the sector and the sphere of activity: people do not like it when something is imposed upon them.'

A significant point in this respect is to encourage the setting-up of the network in a way that brings in the majority of the peripheral actors. Among the three case studies dealing with large companies, only Air Liquide manages to set up the network in a way that truly relates to all the members of the sub-units. At GTIE, for example, the bulk of inter-company relations is dealt with by the company manager and some of the account managers, removing possibilities of 'meshing.' In order for organizational cohesion to result from the network, the phenomenon must go beyond inter-individual relationships to become a collective relationship between units. The fact of affirming – as is done at Air Liquide – that any individual must be able to contact any other individual who holds information and knowledge that he or she requires, whatever his or her position in the organization, is very important in encouraging the opening-up of intra-organizational frontiers.

The center also has an important part to play in creating opportunities to meet among the individuals of the company. It is indeed the center which can set up the structures that make it possible to encourage the emergence of the various clubs, networks or 'study groups' that have already been described. Training events, which are just as much used in the mobilization of clan logic, play a rather similar role of socialization in this respect. The same applies to some meetings organized by the operational or functional management, which are likewise opportunities for extra meetings which can help the development of the network organization to take off. All these mechanisms are particularly well-developed at GTIE, where the regional manager has a very significant role to play in the 'meshing' of the group. Thus, various meetings are organized, beyond those for purposes of budgetary follow-up. A monthly meeting gathers together all the company managers reporting to the same director: 'business is discussed. This allows everyone to reveal his needs. It is there that the competences of the others are called upon.' In addition, thematic seminars can be organized for one region, or even interregional meetings can be set up (in general, one or two meetings per year for a given region). At these meetings, open interaction between members beyond purely formal content is sought after systematically. Furthermore, there are a whole series of meetings that concern the entire group. These meetings are at the same time both an opportunity for the group's management to transmit its messages and a chance for participants to weave bonds with each other. The working groups of GTIE are often quoted together with the clubs. These structures, which are only temporary and more formal, are intended to discuss subjects of general interest for the group. They lead regularly to the drafting of a report. Different training events are also organized for several companies. Those who were interviewed often emphasized the importance of all these tools as tools of socialization. Very often they mentioned in one breath the meetings, the training events, the clubs, and the working groups: 'I take part in a working group on the public market, one of my collaborators takes part in an electro-technical club, and another works with an automation club. We also have two leaders of training courses in technology and automation. It is important for the technical, aspects but also to meet people. One can knit relationships together there.'

Mobilizing the Clan Logic

The center also guarantees cohesion by the clan. The clan is indeed based on a legitimate authority that belongs to the core. The means available to a central unit for encouraging the network organization are very important, thanks to the mechanisms of the clan. Recruitment policy, career management, training as well as the development of broad organizational themes all make it possible to embed the network organization. Air Liquide uses these levers across the board, which proved extremely useful at the time of the introduction to the field of an approach based on initiative and autonomy. The recourse to the clan is quite certainly one of the means of going beyond simply undertaking specific short-term operations. The clan can help to establish a real logic of cooperation, thanks to which it is possible to envisage evolution towards sharing customers, transferring competences, or even a form of collegial governance. However, the clan is above all an essential element in the support of change, particularly in the transition from a way of working in which hierarchical elements are essential to a more cross-cutting mode of operation.

Let us analyze in more detail the way in which the center mobilizes the clan at Air Liquide. There are certain major strategic themes that are regularly put forward in the company. Among these themes, the following come up in particular: the customer and customized service, development and growth of the business, and finally, the importance of initiative in the field. These major themes are brought up frequently, and the goal is to give them content by means of discussion, to come back to them and to reflect on them: 'You bathe in them.' 'These themes are constantly being brought up. During operational meetings one or another of the themes is mentioned... The principal values are referred to regularly during the large meetings, and we rehearse them and discuss them.'

One of the preferred channels of dissemination for these major themes is the vertical axis, consisting of the management committee and the regional managers. The regional manager is indeed an essential wheel. The content of the major themes is widely discussed and analyzed during the meetings that are held at this level. It is then brought up again in the field at every opportunity: 'A meeting takes place every year or every six months over two or three working days with the departmental director and the regional managers. Other collaborators can be included at certain times. Strong messages are passed on at these occasions. Every month there is also an enlarged management committee meeting, with a third of the regional managers. At all of these meetings, the major themes are always brought up. At all team meetings, at every level, these values are referred to.' Finally, there are two company newsletters. In these newsletters it is above all the achievements of people which are highlighted. The comments of one member of the human resources department in this respect are clear: 'The same applies to the company newsletters or the videos showing subsidiaries or activities: the themes come out from the remarks made by people, even by those on the other side of the world. When these values were launched, they were hammered into us systematically, the materials were translated, and sent out everywhere.' It is clear to see, throughout the remarks of these agents, that the power of themes like initiative in the field comes from the capacity of the center to illustrate them constantly, in particular by mobilizing the mechanisms of the clan.

The criteria of recruitment to a large extent stress the possibility of integrating the individual into the structures of the group. Technical skills alone are not the determining factor. Thus the individuals who are recruited are compatible with the group's value system, particularly in terms of initiative and ability to work across boundaries. For the human resources department, this criterion is significant at every level, whether for managers or for those who are not: 'in some cases, we recruit only specialists. In general, we seek generalists, people who can adapt themselves to a variety of functions. It is necessary to have people who communicate: those who are curious, open, autonomous, leaders. They should not be afraid to pass on their knowledge, to communicate laterally. We recruit people who we think can work in a team. The concepts of sharing and generosity are important. This type of concern is also expressed for the non-executives.' Another factor in integration that is particularly emphasized is mobility, which is intense in the group, whether it be occupational mobility or geographic mobility. Generally, there is very little external recruitment and only for posts which require some experience.

Beyond the traditional training activities, Air Liquide also makes use of training on the job. For example, a salesman will accompany another salesman in another region for two months, 'this allows them to make contact and to begin to set up a network.' Training in the workplace, by an 'old hand' is an important element in the transmission of the company's values. Mentoring also plays a definite part. Mentoring is a way of ensuring that newcomers are integrated into the company. Someone in the company is chosen to help the new recruit in his or her work. There is no precise content envisaged in advance. It is simply indicated that the mentor must 'spend time with the person.' The relationship is intentionally very free, is not monitored by any external person, and is not the object of any report. As one worker points out, 'The system of mentoring newcomers must be carried out by somebody who knows the current company culture well, but who also has a good understanding of how the company wants to develop.'

In the development of CFDP we find a significant role played by a center that intervenes according to the clan. The initial vision is placed up-front by the company, and this vision goes well beyond economic profitability; it is concerned to change relationships in the workplace. This desire makes CFDP a unique experiment in which everything happens by emphasizing total autonomy. The delegates clearly express this role of the mission as the engine of the network organization at the instigation of Yves Michel, CFDP's former CEO: 'Yves Michel's desire is to make work no longer just a job. There must be osmosis between professional and personal life. This is supposed to lead to a delegate's happiness, and he or she can then communicate this happiness with others. For this to happen there must be a sharing of power and an apprenticeship.' The propagation of this project depended essentially on its constant assertion by Yves Michel and Michel Plantin (the other original leader of the company). The vision didn't allow any statutory hierarchy, by giving the power to the delegates. It was the two directors of the company who imposed the vision, by encouraging constant questioning within the organization as soon as a hierarchical level appeared: 'All the structures were meant to support a mechanism of understanding, approval and ownership' with regard to the vision. This notion now seems to have been taken up by the Committee of Ethics and Orientation, which is the new guardian of the vision.

Beyond putting the network at the forefront, the clan is essential in the support of individuals who lose their hierarchical reference points with the evolution towards the network. Thus, at Air Liquide, the transition, as experienced by some people, was difficult. Sometimes former managers felt themselves dispossessed of their privileges without being offered any compensation: 'The problem is to know how to give signs of recognition to individuals in a non-hierarchical operation. To some extent, it is necessary to invent recognition.' The dispossession is not always viewed in a positive light, and the motivation lost on the one side is not always found on the other.

Some people question the desire of former subordinates to decide: 'People must agree to make decisions. The structures led to a decrease in motivation of the people in charge but motivated only some of the subordinates (some protected themselves)... It was perhaps going a little too quickly for the family atmosphere at Air Liquide.' 'Some people know how to work autonomously; others do not, whatever their level. Some workers are excellent at making decisions concerning their job, but there are top-of-the-range salespeople who regularly demand approval from the regional sales manager or the regional manager. Difficulties appear because some people do not want to make decisions.' The systematic valuation of expertise played a significant role in the transition to the network at Air Liquide. However, here again, changing the status of manager to one of expert is not always easy. The role is ambiguous. Some experts who do not have any hierarchical privileges distinguish themselves de facto by their role in the region: 'My role depends on the behaviour of people, I feel good about it. It is difficult to be an advisor in both directions; that is to say, towards the director and towards the others. I am nonetheless a department head because I am in contact most frequently with the boss.'

Through these reactions, it is easy to see the importance of the center's role as a force in proposing a new system of values within which the actors will be able to find their reference points. This guiding, supportive role is essential if one wants a dynamic network to see the light of day.

THE AREAS OF INTERVENTION

The center can or must also preserve a certain number of areas in which its intervention is desirable or even necessary. First of all, it can be forced to stand in for the peripheral units when they do not want to make a decision. Secondly, there are factors that can only be handled by a central unit. The center can also be considered as a group of experts that operate on the level of advice, rather than by command.

Standing In For Peripheral Units and Representing Them

There are some cases in which the peripheral units do not want or are not able to make a decision. A central unit has to take over in such cases. The coolness of the peripheral actors with regard to collective decision-making has been established. They still hang onto the hope of centralized decision-making, at least on certain issues. The peripheral actors are indeed more worried about carrying out their local strategic plan than about decisions that affect the entire group.

For this reason, CFDP adopted a principle of subsidiarity: the center intervenes if the peripheral units do not wish to make decisions any longer. This fundamental principle of subsidiarity thus consists in handling at the lowest level everything that can be handled there, and transferring the other problems to a higher level. Certain issues that relate to the entire company must be approached globally, for example, relations with a big national insurance company for which they handle a nation-wide contract or with the national insurance committee (the controlling body of the business). However, 'the Inter-Regional Committee intervenes as little as possible.' According to the urgency and the importance of the decision to be made, the twinned pairs of the Inter-Regional Committee can replace the teams and make a decision by themselves: 'Each twinned pair of the IRC has the power to decide in the name of the IRC when the team or region does not want to do so. They generally consult the other members of the IRC and the CEO (Committee on Ethics and Orientation) on topics that involve ethics or strategy.'

There is a role that the center must be able to continue to play: that of arbitrator of the conflicts between units. In the majority of the cases, the adjustments between units are autonomous; the management of interdependencies does not require intervention by the center. Moreover, if a cooperative relationship is really established, it should be possible to avoid the majority of conflicts. Nevertheless, sources of discord or confrontations between units always exist, whether they are in good or bad faith. It is thus important that the central actors be able to play the role of arbitrator.

The intervention of the center can also be imposed by external agents. The company must have exterior representation, and certain external actors might wish to meet a person 'with authority.' The relationships with shareholders can come up against this type of constraint. The same applies to a banker, a particularly significant customer, or a public body. Thus, after installing the new structures and launching the project of repurchase of a part of the capital by the delegates, CFDP anticipated that it would name a chairman who could undertake this representative role.

On the other hand, the majority of the functional activities can be handled by specialized peripheral units, which provide support to other units. Thus the need to concentrate one particular resource can be satisfied without requiring the return to a bureaucratic approach. So it does not seem necessary to centralize or to exercise control to obtain concentrated management of resources. As has been shown, Air Liquide excels in the practice of this art and has successfully increased the number of support units, which appear as specialized peripheral units. Another possibility is to externalize all specialized functions. This is the choice made by CFDP.

The Expert Centre

The peripheral units can also recognize the value of a high level of expertise in the center. If this condition holds, command is no longer necessary, and the peripheral actors quite naturally come to solicit the advice and help of a center with strong legitimacy. This legitimacy gives the center the possibility of making a certain number of decisions without being seen as constraining by the peripheral units. Career paths which require a person to prove him or herself in the field before taking part in central activities can be useful in this respect. They make it possible to put together a central unit made up of credible individuals. Moreover, as an agency manager at Colas points out, if the central actors have real knowledge of the business and of the pressures on the field, it is quite probable that they will come to make decisions that accord with the periphery's expectations. A true respect for the expert and expertise is found in three of the cases studied. At Air Liquide, a significant effort is made to avoid a statutory hierarchy in favor of recognized expertise. In the same way, knowledge of the business by the center at Colas ensures the legitimacy of the decisions made. At CFDP also, the Committee on Ethics and Orientation gathers together actors recognized for their expertise. The substitution of respect for expertise for authoritarian decision-making goes clearly in the direction of the network organization.

Thus, with Air Liquide, the main functional management teams draw their legitimacy from their knowledge. They are 'super-experts,' as we were told in one interview. For this reason, they are regularly brought into problems that need to be handled with delicacy: 'If a problem appears, I can seek opinions, recommendations. That makes it possible to take on the acquired knowledge of my neighbors. If I have an unusual subject to deal with, I ask the regional director; he generally has the answer, and if not, he can turn to other regional directors.' The operational personnel that we met all highlighted the importance of this central expertise; for one management head, 'Relations with the central accounting departments are frequent. They have a role of support and advice, and they also make us comply with the accounting rules... they are specialists in the accounting profession. Their role is that of certified accountants.' For a regional director of customer relations, 'with a complicated problem, we are happy to have support with regard to a precise field. There is little intervention on their part. It is especially for help and advice. The desire is that they should be at our disposal.'

In the same line of thinking, at Colas, the operational managers of the subsidiary are always there for support; the idea here is for agency managers to benefit from their competence. For difficult or risky deals, exchanges are frequent between the head office of the subsidiary company and the agency managers: 'In difficult sectors, contact is frequent. The logic is that of help and not of control. Help is also given on commercial, administrative, and technical issues.' The functional management teams must similarly play this role of service provider with respect to the agencies and sub-subsidiary companies in many fields. The general rule is that of support to the head of the agency. For example, a director of human resources in a subsidiary company describes his role like this: 'If it is necessary to dismiss someone, we provide technical support, but we do not do it in the place of the agency manager... Alain Dupont[28] says, "the truth is in the agencies." He is right, we are there to help them, not to annoy them. It would be impossible to do otherwise.'

28. Alain Dupont is the CEO of Colas.

7. Organizational cohesion

The four companies which the reader has come to know throughout these chapters all devote an important place to the network within their organization. If we return to the initial problem posed in this work, however, we recall that the network is only one of the organizational logics that can explain the cohesion of an organization. The opening postulate went so far as to say that in any organization the network coexists to a greater or lesser extent with the market, the bureaucracy, or the clan: one of the basic principles of the conceptual framework is that of the multiplicity of modes of organization simultaneously present in a given organization.

Thus, in all the situations that have been studied, other principles combine with the network and have a part in this cohesion. The delimitation of the center's role, described in the preceding chapter, was a first approach to the intermingling of the different modes of organization. This combination is more or less easy. Tensions and contradictions can appear between the modes of organization: the network is opposed to the non-cooperative approach of the market, as well as to the hierarchical character of bureaucracy and the clan. But beyond such tensions, the companies studied knew how to find a balance that called for different use of the four modes of organization.

First of all, this chapter presents an assessment of the way in which Air Liquide, CFDP, Colas and GTIE mobilize the four modes of organization in order to establish their cohesion. This synthesis illustrates the possibilities which the book's conceptual framework offers for drawing up an operational diagnosis. Then comes a cross-cutting analysis of the way in which the three other modes of organization (the market, the bureaucracy, and the clan) combine with the network. This shows how reinforcements of cohesion or, conversely, deadlocks can appear between the network and the other modes of organization. These analyses lead to more general conclusions about organizational cohesion.

WHAT COHESION FOR THE FOUR COMPANIES?

Each company found its own balance, using a specific combination of the four modes of organization. These balances are described here in a synthetic analysis of the organizational cohesion for each case.

Between Clan and Network: Air Liquide

Market mechanisms are rarely used within Air Liquide, where the clan and the network are particularly emphasized. Bureaucracy is more or less mobilized depending upon the peripheral unit concerned. On the other hand, there is always the will to develop, firstly, a feeling of belonging to the group, and, secondly, autonomous exchanges between units centered around a specific activity.

Competition between Air Liquide's sub-units is non-existent: the distribution of activities, whether geographical or by trade, makes any competition improbable. On the other hand, there are many transfers between units. These transfers are frequent and relate both to significant volumes and to a large number of products. They concern the internal sales of gas first of all, but also transfers of material: cylinders, cryogenic tanks, or even units for gas conditioning. However, this internal market is not very realistic. Prices are actually negotiated between managements and are then imposed on the sub-units. Even if these prices include a margin for the sub-units that supply the product or the equipment, no real confrontation with the market takes place. Market mechanisms thus play a relatively weak role in the cohesion of the group, as the policy is always to use internal products and services even if they are more expensive than those proposed by competitors.

Organization by bureaucracy is present within the group. It is appropriate, however, to qualify this assessment depending on the unit in which one is interested. The control exercised by the center is indeed much more evident for the industrial plants than for the regions. The regions benefit from a more significant margin of maneuver without being subjected to strong pressure on controlling results.

For the regions, various tools for control by input are used. The strategic plan, as well as the budget that is associated with it, are the object of in-depth collaborative work. This involves a real discussion during which consensus is sought. Functional coordination also plays a significant role. The weight of this functional coordination remains very moderate, however, and it relates primarily to non-debatable fields like security or legal aspects. Moreover, since the central units are viewed as 'super-experts,' contacts are frequent with the regions which benefit from the help and advice of these central units. The center also intervenes to fix the rules of transfer between the units and plays a rather strong role in matters of resource allocation: investment is monitored. However, in this matter, the regional directors do not perceive any constraint on their development. In every case, it involves control that is not very restrictive and that is intended to help and support the regions rather than to direct them. As for transfers of expertise, they are managed directly between the units.

In the same spirit, control by results is not very restrictive. It is clear that an individual who acts contrary to common sense cannot hope for a brilliant career profile within the group. However, the margin of error seems real, and there is not any worship of numbers or results in any case. In the event of a problem, the regional director must explain himself. Monitoring is done by exception, and discrepancies are allowed if they are explained. In addition, the objectives are at the same time both quantitative and qualitative: it is the balance between the two that is judged. As we showed in the last chapter, clan mechanisms are widely used at Air Liquide. All the tools are used to support the feeling of belonging to the group, as well as for diffusing major themes or values.

The recruitment policy favors the capacity to integrate into the group rather than technical skill. The human resources department takes part in the recruitment of executives and then monitors their careers regularly. Mobility is desirable, and they try to hire young people who will stay within the group. Every opportunity is used 'to hammer home' the company's major themes. At all of the field or management meetings, as well as during training events, discussions and reflection are launched on these major themes. It is not simply a matter of announcing them when the opportunity presents itself, but also involves encouraging individuals to take ownership of these themes by making them reflect on them. The two company newsletters are also vehicles for these guiding themes. Last of all, the final tool of integration into the group is the system of mentoring, which also encourages the informal transmission of a certain number of values.

Air Liquide's peripheral units have various activities and roles. They are strongly interdependent and many network mechanisms are mobilized within the group. There are many significant possibilities and they are often used. Some of the peripheral units are designed to carry out projects in collaboration with the regions. This is the case for the Floxal units (on-site production), the CEPIAs (development centers) and the service team. The regions have access to their resources, whether it be technical skills for the Floxal teams and the CEPIAs or carrying out tests by the CEPIAs. The development managers (attached to the CEPIAs) and members of the Floxal teams are associated with the projects of the regions. They manage the overall steering of the implementation of the project or can intervene as internal advisors. In all cases, mixed teams can be set up to respond to the request of a particular customer. The bonds existing between the support units and the regions are very rich and of course include relationships of mutual aid and advice but also reciprocal influence and control.

Furthermore, there are many transfers between the units. These transfers primarily concern gas but also concern equipment, in particular storage equipment. As we have seen, there is no real market relationship between the units. On the other hand, adjustments of quantities and deliveries are dealt with across units. For these activities to go well, trust between members is necessary: trust at the level of the demands made by each one and in the pertinence of the deadlines requested. So, the adjustment of transactions is more a matter of organization by the network than organization by the market. These transfers take place without any particular difficulty and in a climate of shared trust.

Exchanges are easily made between the peripheral units of the group. The logic proposed is that of free access to a qualified interlocutor, whatever the position of the person seeking information. The very flexible networks set up by the group allow such exchanges for most of the people in the regions. It is essential to note that these networks develop without the constraint of results: they are not held to account. Free exchange and a rich discussion can thus take place, and these networks serve as an opportunity to help new ideas emerge. The bonds of contact, help, and advice observed between the peripheral units of various natures confirm the possibilities offered by autonomous exchange at this level.

Collegiality in decision-making is not really emphasized within the group. Thus, the formulation of the Department's strategic objectives follows a top-down path; but, at the same time, there is a desire to draw out ideas and information from the field, and to multiply the opportunities for consulting the peripheral units. In this spirit, working groups allow the development of plans concerning the entire organization, whether by actors from the periphery or by others.

The Almost Total Network: CFDP

The cohesion of CFDP depends above all on the network. This mode of organization is largely dominant. There is a certain role played by the clan in affirming the vision. Bureaucracy is marginal if one compares CFDP with the other companies studied, and the market does not intervene in the regulation of the company's internal relationships.

The case of CFDP is undoubtedly the one in which the market plays the least significant role in the company's internal cohesion. It can even be noted that this goes for the relationships between the company and its principal customers too, since the relationships with intermediaries rely even more heavily upon partnership. There is no transfer between delegates, and this is not desired. There is also no competition possible between delegates responsible for the development of the company in a given geographical sector. The market thus plays no part in the cohesion of the company.

Control by results is also non-existent within the company. Performance indicators for monthly follow-ups were recently developed by the Inter-Regional Committee (IRC). There was no objective negotiated or proposed by the center and the variable part of pay was allocated to the team as if it were independent of actual performance. On the other hand, a limited control by input is present. The allocation of resources is completely free. However, after discussion, the IRC can impose certain decisions in fields which have effects on the whole company. This applies to hiring, for example.

The study of CFDP's development shows the difficulties of operating in a logic of extreme autonomy. The period in which the company was searching for an adapted collegial structure is particularly indicative in this respect. The absence of bureaucratic organization, insofar as another mode of organization did not take over from it, made for a significant risk of disorganization for the company, which lost cohesion. On the other hand, such a structure can be an example of real flexibility once it has found its balance.

CFDP's plan does not hide its cultural content. Its leaders' objective during its launching was clearly to bring about attachment to the vision, attachment to a system of values different from those usually prevailing in the corporate world. There is even a desire to propagate this system of values beyond the frontiers of the company. The role of the two leaders has now been taken over primarily by the EOC (Ethics and Orientation Committee), which assures the continuation of the vision. The CIR also plays a role in relaying company values, because its decisions are made with constant care to reflect the goals of the vision.

The criteria of recruitment applied within the company strongly emphasize the 'socializability' of the candidates and not their technical skill. The technical skill most often used by the representatives is that relating to law. However, there are very few lawyers in the company. Recruitment focuses primarily on consultants: what is desired is their capacity easily to take part in a vision in which autonomy plays an essential role. Recruitment is carried out directly by the delegates, with the desire to continue the vision. Integration of newcomers is done within the team; an induction period of about one year is needed. Legal competences are acquired during this time. The essential element in the cohesion of the company is clearly the network, throughout the search for a collegial form.

There are joint projects between several sets of representatives, whether or not they belong to the same team. In most cases, they concern the development of a new service for the intermediaries. These projects, however, remain relatively rare. On the other hand, the transfer of skills seems easier. It is very simple to obtain information, an explanation of the solution to a problem. The relationships between delegations are very rich and often include bonds of mutual aid and advice, but they are also relationships of trust.

It is clearly in its search for a form of collegial structure that CFDP distinguishes itself from the other companies. After trying out six different structures in fifteen years, the company has succeeded in finding a balance. If the experience of CFDP shows us the possibilities offered by the network, it also highlights the difficulties of such an exercise. On this point, the fact of the introduction of the insurance intermediaries to the internal meetings made it possible for the delegates to progress very quickly to improve the collegial structure. The intermediaries indeed play the primary role of a mirror, facilitating decision-making and making it easier for the delegates to set the direction of their decisions.

Colas: A Balance Between Clan, Network and Bureaucracy

The integration of the peripheral units takes place at Colas largely by means of a strong combination of clan and network. The actors from the peripheral environment of the agencies play a particularly important role in the coherence of their development. The bureaucratic mechanisms subscribe to an approach that tries as a whole to encourage the autonomy of the peripheral units, but still there is a bureaucratic pressure within the firm. The contribution of market mechanisms to the organization of the group is less marked.

The market does not play a determining role in the cohesion of the group. On the one hand, the agencies are not in competition; it cannot be envisaged that they would respond to the same invitation to tender. Moreover, there is no opportunity for carrying out joint projects between agencies and consequently no need for coordination by the market at this level. The only reference to the market might relate to the transfer of equipment and teams between the agencies. These exchanges are quite frequent, but the prices of the transfers, calculated by the center, correspond to a logic of cost implications and not to market prices. In addition, the agencies must always choose to use the group's equipment, even if this costs them, on analysis, more than equipment coming from outside the group. Neither do the transfers between the agencies and the Large Works Unit call upon the mechanisms of the market.

Bureaucratic aspects have some importance in Colas' organizational coherence but these aspects are built into a logic of independence. The influences of planning and control thus are always very moderate, and intervention by command is exceptional. The peripheral units are much more worried about the need to meet the expectations of their customers than about the demands of people from the subsidiary's head office, which are deliberately not very weighty.

The control by results exercised by the center is relatively flexible. Budgets are above all regarded as management tools which make it possible to comprehend the situation better, to forecast results and to react in the event of a blunder. Control is flexible, and it is understood that the trade is subject to uncontrollable risks, or that the competitive context can justify a fall in profitability.

Control by input is more marked; however, it is concerned with a wish for constructiveness, joint reflection, and advice. Moreover, this type of control is exerted by individuals who have real experience in the trade and so are able truly to bring help. The agency managers retain a preponderant influence in this process. Some factors are, however, imposed, factors which concern the whole of the group and their common interest.

The convergence of values is one of the essential factors in the organizational cohesion of the company. It rests in large part on the road construction profession, on common experience; the management of human resources has attracted particularly marked attention, where one finds the desire to have strong integration at all stages of career development.

Thus, the criteria of recruitment put particular emphasis on factors concerning relationships; technical aspects are not determining factors. The bulk of recruitment is aimed at young people whose careers are monitored very attentively, with the aim of ensuring their development within the group. Internal mobility, an important element of socialization, is regularly required by means of changes of job. Furthermore, there is a package of training whose content is carefully chosen and where a superior takes part regularly in parts concerning the major themes of the group. These themes are taken up in meetings at all levels, as well as in the company newsletter; they include safety and quality, but above all the desire for professionalism in road construction, associated with respect for others. One can find the values associated with the trade in the internal relationships within the units, where the respect for experienced people is very pronounced. Thus, individuals having a managerial role are also those to whom one comes to seek help and especially those whom one trusts to regulate sensitive professional problems. The center thus exerts a significant influence while enabling strong socialization of individuals within the company.

The peripheral units are very clearly compartmentalized, as each agency is particularly involved in penetrating its local networks. There are thus few or no decisions made jointly, nor having a general range, and the transmission of expertise seems difficult. The only bonds between units relate to exchanges of equipment and teams. If these exchanges are brought up in conversation, they do not engender frequent contact and deeper relationships between the units. This observation shows a lack of work across boundaries within the group, but it also indicates the facility with which exchanges can take place autonomously between peripheral units, without the intervention of the center.

The image globally conveyed by Colas is a resource shared between units. It is partly created at group level, but each agency answers for it too, and there is strong interdependence in this respect. Image thus appears to be a resource created jointly, according with the phenomenon of emergence. On the other hand, some cohesion is brought about by recourse to departments of head office, which present themselves as a body of common resources. In all cases where the agencies request the support of head office, one cannot speak of bureaucratic organization, and yet the fact of using the same service provider reinforces organizational cohesion considerably.

In addition, branches are strongly open to their local environment: there is a significant breaking down of barriers with respect to competitors and a relationship based on intimacy and collaborative work with the customer. This case highlights the importance that can be vested in external control and influence, conveyed primarily by the customers. Customers and suppliers, by the influence they exert on the agencies, thus seem to be key actors in integrating the agencies and in producing coherence in the development of the group. The opening of the frontiers of the sub-units to their local environment contributes strongly to an emerging convergence: it is a matter of doing the same job in relation to similar external actors and in geographical areas of similar sizes.

The Combination of Market and Network: GTIE

The organizational cohesion of GTIE depends primarily on a combination of market and network. The market provides the rules of the game for working as a network of similar 'companies' that are moreover connected very strongly to their customers. The group's organization as a bureaucracy appears as a backcloth: it primarily concerns the heads of the companies who nevertheless maintain a significant margin of maneuver.

Among the cases studied, GTIE is certainly the one for which the market plays the most significant role in organizing the relationships between units. Competition between units is not sought. On the contrary, transfers are numerous and regularly require the use of market mechanisms. The company's projects are conceived in such a way as to avoid competition in downstream markets and there is consensus on this point within the group. Examples of conflict to win the same customer are thus few and are generally settled directly by the companies. On the other hand, transactions between companies are current practice within the group and are strongly encouraged. They can be frequent and of high volume. Prices are always negotiated freely between them and include the units' normal margins. Market mechanisms go even further: the group's companies are very often made to compete by their internal customers, who do not hesitate to accept a less expensive proposition originating from outside the group. There is thus real continuity between the internal market and the external market with internal transactions contributing in the same way as external transactions to the results of the unit.

Cohesion by bureaucracy within GTIE is based more on control by results than on control by input. Another characteristic is that the pressure of output control is exerted though an exclusive bond with the head of each company. Where control by input is concerned, the center intervenes very little in the coordination of activities between peripheral units. It limits itself to imposing the rule of the market, to encouraging the use of the network and to intervening in cases of conflict. In the same way, apart from general constraints linked to the financial equilibrium of the group, the center intervenes very little in investment policies. It leaves a large part of their self-financing capacity to the companies. The influence of the center is expressed primarily through the discussion of strategic planning and by exchanges between the regional manager and the head of the company. However, the plan is not imposed, and the exchanges with the regional manager aim to find consensual solutions to the problems encountered by the company managers.

The quantitative part of the budget and the objectives associated with it correspond to a set of relatively light financial criteria. However, real pressure exists to obtain and improve results; very detailed monitoring is carried out each month. Error is allowed, but this right is limited. Moreover, a significant part of the chief executive's remuneration depends on achievement of the objectives.

It is surprising to note how little the clan is put into action within GTIE. Several actors at various levels of the organization affirmed this: the feeling of belonging to the company dominates the feeling of belonging to the group.

The center intervenes very little in recruitment, and there is no set standard of criteria. Mobility within the group is weak. An individual makes his career primarily within the company. Some training schemes are managed by the center; however, their objective is technical training or meeting other members of the group rather than the diffusion of values. Generally speaking, big assemblies and other meetings are seen as opportunities to meet other individuals from the group. The important messages in fact are primarily used to encourage other organizational modes. They are calls to knit together to develop the network and strong messages about obtaining results.

There are undoubtedly exchanges and significant possibilities of joint implementation between the companies of the group. However, inter-individual recurrent relations are often limited to the heads of companies and possibly to their direct collaborators.

The first element in the network organization is the implementation of joint projects. The companies of GTIE call upon internal subcontractors or joint contractors. This point is regarded as strategic for maintaining the competitiveness of the group. Companies engaging in such an approach show a real capacity for recombining their structures: they can easily create new structures ad hoc. Joint projects are launched when the companies are insufficiently large or, more frequently and more easily, if the project makes use of complementary competences. A second element is that of the exchange of personnel to compensate for periods of work underload. Equipment can also easily be exchanged. It is particularly interesting to note that all these exchanges are made without intervention of the center: the companies are free to work together or not, and all the adjustments are autonomous. The regional managers are responsible for too many companies to guide the interdependencies, and their intervention is seen as undesirable.

However, it seems difficult to go as far as the stage of implementing projects that do not fall directly within the objective of immediate profitability. Working groups and clubs exist but they are in fact few and involve only a limited number of people. One may then doubt their capacity to decide general questions together. Relationships follow a logic of profitability, with doing business as the principal objective; knowledge sharing per se comes only afterwards and less often.

THE NETWORK AND THE OTHER MODES OF ORGANIZATION

The four organizational modes are divided two by two according to the two dimensions which structure the conceptual framework: cooperation/non-cooperation, hierarchy/non-hierarchy. They are therefore opposed conceptually. However, one finds each organizational mode in all four of the companies studied. The life of organizations allows for a combination of the organizational modes to a certain extent. We thus have to better understand the way in which the network is connected with the other modes of organization; we analyze here the risks and also the advantages, tied to the combination of the network with each organizational mode.

The Network and the Market

Our four companies use market mechanisms essentially in two ways. The first type of market relationship, seen particularly at Air Liquide and GTIE, concerns transactions between the units. It appears in this case that the reference to the market must be nuanced if one wants to avoid contradiction on the cooperation/non-cooperation axis. Indeed, an overly pronounced reference to the market disturbs some of the possibilities offered by the network, while the absence of any reference can lead to dysfunction and a loss of confidence towards the internal partner. The second type of market mechanism which is used is that of competition between units. This type of approach damages cooperation between the units and thus very quickly becomes detrimental to the network organization. Table 7.1 summarizes the results concerning the combination of network and market.

Table 7.1 The network and the market

MARKET	PURPOSE OF THE COMBINATION	RISKS	POSSIBLE RESPONSES
Transfers	• Allows exchanges	• Negotiation instead of cooperation	• Confronting external markets • Benchmarking towards competitors' offers
Competition	• Augmenting market share	• Competition instead of cooperation	• Non-recovery for projects of the peripheral units

Reference to the market is frequent within the framework of transfers between the units. If one reconsiders the various dimensions of the network mode of organization, one finds: the exchange of equipment or teams, the sale of products and the implementation of joint projects in which one or more units are billed for their services. Choices must be made about the management and accounting for such operations, since organization by the network is generally not sufficient for the management of large operations that have major consequences for the results of the peripheral units. The problem that arises is that of the distribution of profits between the units: the market can in this case then provide an answer. The two possible ways of referring to the market are rather well represented by the cases of GTIE and

Air Liquide. Colas is close to Air Liquide in its exchanges between regions and to GTIE, without going so far as setting up competition for projects carried out with the diversified subsidiary companies (SES and Somaro).

In the first case, that of GTIE, reference to the market is very strong. All transactions between companies take place at the market rate. The hours are invoiced internally as hours of service provided to external clients and include overheads and a margin. As we have indicated, the companies of the group have the possibility – and they frequently resort to it – of putting the internal units into competition with companies outside the group. The group's peripheral units are, for certain services, regularly put into such competition and are not necessarily chosen, without any possibility of assessing the consequences of this behavior for the whole group. Negotiations are thus sometimes bitter between the companies of the group. Depending on the nature of the relationships between the units, the internal units are or are not made to compete with companies outside the group: 'We do not do them any favors, but we give them the market, we do not seek elsewhere,' 'Some regularly seek the best price; so for some services we are no longer even consulted.' In other situations, preference is given to the units of the group, meantime keeping some check on the prices charged. The internal subcontractor often knows the price suggested by the competitors and can reduce his tender: 'When other [internal] companies call on us, they generally tell us the gap between our prices and those of our competitors and ask us to adjust accordingly, which we cannot always do.' The fact that another company of the group is experiencing slack in its workload can be taken into account, but a company's manager will not, in the name of overall profitability, take on business at a loss. On this matter, the actors are rather eloquent: 'In any case, this is happening between people who know each other, but one cannot require them to lose money. What takes priority is carrying out the workload within GTIE, then comes profitability.' 'The logic is that of the market: we mustn't be in deficit.'

Such dealing, in which the market plays an important role, can lead to unexpected difficulties after the event. It then becomes necessary, just as in an external network, to learn to work together and to provide formal contingency measures to be used as a safety net. As one company manager said: 'Within the group, I thought that it would be as if I had asked two account executives to muck in together in my company, but it is more difficult... In my experience, compared to my competitors, we formalize a lot. We thought about it too little within the group, and so problems appeared afterwards. The group preens itself on its close relationships, everyone wants them, but fear remains.'

The use of competition seems to be accepted as the way in which the group works; but it is also perceived as the drawback of a method based on autonomy: 'One cannot abandon autonomy and just say go talk to someone; this sets a limit to the method.' Some emphasize its stimulating aspect while others regret missed opportunities for collaboration: 'Competition stimulates: it obliges one to be competitive, if not, the internal client finds himself losing money. It is a real market.' 'The relationship is that of the market, but what bothers me is that our colleagues subcontract from outside instead of calling on us.' The rare cases of the center's intervention correspond to excessive competition. In the following case, a company in the group was not consulted: 'From time to time, the managing director can even intervene if things go too far. Business which could have been subcontracted to us had gone to another company. We were not aware of this, and our company was in a slack period. We were warned by suppliers. It was a large order that demanded high technical ability, but we were put into competition with people who weren't serious. The case made its way up to the managing director. It is abnormal not to consult in-house for such a big technical operation when we had spare capacity. In normal business, there is no intervention, even if there is a problem.'

In cases where preference is not given to the units of the group, the problems arising from this system are numerous. Firstly, it introduces a non-cooperative relationship between the peripheral units. This state of mind can inhibit less directly remunerative cooperation (canvassing for customers, transfer of skills, and collegiality). Resort to market mechanisms thus reinforces a tendency to take into account only the shared operations which have a clearly identifiable financial interest in the short term. One can even suppose that tensions resulting from the excessive use of the market will disturb the trust necessary to undertake common activities. Moreover, the market reinforces the rather natural tendency to opportunism, or at least the tendency to put the company's interest before that of the group as a whole.

The market plays a much less marked role in the organization of Air Liquide. There is no direct negotiation of price between peripheral units: delivery prices are negotiated at the central level. The internal supplier in Air Liquide is an exclusive supplier. The problem of performance now arises. Indeed, several actors mentioned the fact that it was possible to buy supplies from outside the group at a lower price. Some people complained about the internal delivery price for products: 'The only factors on which the regions cannot act are the prices of products in bulk and of air gases... We accept this and see corresponding revenues from what Air Liquide has conceded to us. Some can be a little sour... a regional director doesn't say, "If it is not competitive, I buy it from the competitor." ' 'The limit is when the product becomes unsaleable.' The idea was recently born of introducing reference to the market in the evaluation of the manufacturing units. The pressure of the external market is then exerted in-house without rupturing the cooperative relationship between internal suppliers and customers. This solution looks promising in Air Liquide's case, but it is not always feasible. Indeed, in many industries it is not possible to consult competing companies indefinitely without ever signing a contract with them – for instance, in many of GTIE's businesses. In such cases, certainty about the competitiveness of the in-house prices charged implies a need to work with external suppliers.

Another possibility is that the downstream market can be a good source of evaluation of an internal supplier's performance. The reaction of the customer is obviously an indicator that can work very well, particularly in industries that use calls for tender: if the tender is accepted, it means that the group's proposal is competitive with the prices found on the market. The constraint of the market is integrated in this way at Colas. In particular, this is the case for projects involving cooperation between the diversified units and the roadwork subsidiaries. The diversified units concern trades such as safety equipment and road signs and markings. On some projects a joint response from these various trades and those of road construction can be required. In such a case, the Colas agencies generally go through the subsidiary companies of the group, and the pressure comes from the final buyer: 'They are obliged to lower their prices on their contributions because their proposal is integrated into the bid. If I want to go through someone else, nobody will say anything about it, I can do it. In my opinion, one goes through them because they are the leaders. They are part of the group and are the best.' Here, the pressure exerted by external customers on the bid made by the internal suppliers can clearly be seen. Moreover, mechanisms like those of the clan or bureaucracy can help to limit the opportunism of internal agents. Under such conditions, the pressure of the market can be exerted without disturbing the cooperative bonds between the units of the group.

Thus recourse to the market, even though it is sometimes useful in support of transfers between units and the implementation of joint projects, can disturb the trust needed if the network is to cohere. This spelling out of the relationship between market and network makes it possible, however, to highlight three principal mechanisms for producing a network market combination which do not call cooperation into question. Firstly, the external client can exert direct pressure within the framework of joint projects. Customer sanctions are a strong incentive. Secondly, if the internal suppliers also carry out activity for external customers, the market prices are known, and their internal practices can be influenced by their external ones. Lastly, in some cases, information about competitors' supply prices is available and can serve as a standard for internal transactions.

The market can also play a part in the organization of internal relationships by introducing competition between the units. This phenomenon is found within the framework of the Colas group where the sub-subsidiary companies operate under their own brand name: the Sacer and Colas agencies are in direct competition in the same geographical areas. The peripheral units operating under the Colas name are not in competition. It cannot be envisaged that they should respond to the same invitation to tender: the effect on the customer would be disastrous. However, Sacer and Colas do not have any links at the level of the operational unit, and their relationship is organized essentially around the logic of the market. The two groups share certain values because of their common general management. Nevertheless, these are not very decisive factors in comparison with the very harsh competition that can reign in some sectors between two sub-units, one from Colas and one from Sacer. Organization is thus primarily through the market, and competition is very strong at this level: 'Sacer is like a normal competitor; the fighting can be worse in some cases.' The sub-subsidiary companies are more integrated into the operation of the regional subsidiaries. Their directors take part in the meetings of the agency heads held by regional management, and they draw upon the same service functions. On the other hand, there is no sharing of the market, and central management refuses to intervene except in extreme cases of bilateral price war between agencies and sub-subsidiaries: 'There can be competition, the chairman [at the regional level] can be obliged to decide, but he doesn't like doing that. ... We do business together as with other competitors.' There is thus a real war of competition within the group in certain sectors, and the center does not intervene except in extreme cases. The desired effect here is to increase the market-share at the group level. Links between branches are thus not encouraged. This type of relationship takes a directly opposite course to cohesion through the network: cohesion only comes from the association of market and bureaucratic mechanisms. As we have seen, cohesion by the network is destroyed to such an extent by internal competition that in some sectors, the Colas branches more readily undertake building works jointly with a competitor who does not belong to the group, rather than with a Sacer agency.

In the three other companies studied, competition is not sought between the peripheral units, and it is for this reason that organization by the network is possible. The absence of overlap between the peripheral units' strategic projects guarantees the absence of head-on competition between these units, and thus appears to be an essential factor in allowing the type of cooperative relationship that characterizes organizational cohesion based on the network. However, it seems that maintaining the absence of competition between the units is not always an easy exercise. GTIE's situation is particularly enlightening in this matter; problems of opportunism may well appear. These problems can also arise when market mechanisms are used to regulate transactions between companies. Company plans are normally conceived in such a way as to avoid the competitions of two companies for the same customer. However, when the companies undertake similar activities or the same activity in different zones, ambiguity can give rise to a certain mistrust: 'Fear arises from the fact that the group covers all of France: the networking (i.e. implementation of joint projects) runs the risk of making a company come to an area where it does not belong. What works best are the responses by complementary activities. Problems are more difficult when the activities are the same.' 'The reception is often favorable in our case, because our trade is different from the activity of the remainder of the group: we are thus not in the same market as the other companies in the group [...] Things are not as easy with subsidiaries which are slightly closer competitors.' Despite the precautions taken, there are exceptional cases in which two companies respond to the same invitation to tender and are thus in direct competition. In these extreme cases, it is interesting to note that the principle of autonomy is not called into question. Generally, the companies manage the problem themselves and avoid bidding too low: 'In the rare cases of confrontation, adjustments are made directly between the companies within GTIE.' 'If we both canvas, locality plays a part, as well as the fact of having already worked with the customer. We avoid resorting to arbitration from general management and deal with it at our own level.' 'It can happen that we enter into competition, but we try to avoid two answers. We try to be 'big boys.' The problems are handled directly, but there can be cases in which the director intervenes, why not? Competition is not very desirable and does not enter into [our] policy. There are cases where this is done knowingly.' This analysis of GTIE shows both the difficulties encountered in defining projects and the possibilities offered by mutual adjustment mechanisms, network mechanisms to solve problems resulting from being thrown into unwanted competition. The basis of internal avoidance of competition is always the clear definition of each company's project, which avoids overlap. In the absence of such a definition, cohesion by means of the network is called fundamentally into question.

The Network and the Bureaucracy

Organization by bureaucracy is placed opposite to organization by network in our initial conceptual framework: it has its basis in a hierarchical, non-cooperative approach. One might expect to find a marked, systematic opposition between bureaucracy and network. However, as in the case of the market, these two modes of organization coexist, sometimes even happily: it is all a question of proportion. Organization by bureaucracy rests on two main dimensions: control by input and control by output. Too much control by input clearly compromises the autonomy necessary to the network organization, particularly if it bears on the coordination of interdependencies between peripheral units. On the other hand, the center can support the network organization by defining its rules and encouraging its implementation. With regard to control by output, control that is too marked introduces a preoccupation with short-term profit, which destroys any cooperation between the units. On the other hand, the tools of control by output are necessary management tools, and collective objectives can be put in place. Table 7.2 summarizes results concerning the combination of network and bureaucracy.

Table 7.2 The network and the bureaucracy

BUREAUCRACY	OBJECTIVE OF THE COMBINATION	RISKS	POSSIBLE RESPONSES
Interventions	• Encouraging coherence • Limits competition • Encourages working across boundaries	• Loss of autonomy • Impediments to working across boundaries	• Marking out the limits of projects • Assuring the implementation of the network • Setting the rules of interaction
Pressures on profitability	• Profitable autonomy	• Limits long-term operations • The unit's interests come before collective interests • Concealing the customer orientation	• Management tools rather than tools of control • Use of goals linked to the general interest

The implementation of control by input can take two distinct forms both of which can interfere with the logic of the network. It can firstly mean a loss of autonomy for the periphery. It is clear that the network is founded on the absence of hierarchy, on autonomy granted to the peripheral units. If the center takes control of the units' activities, there is no longer any room for organization by the network. Cross-unit activity which could have existed falls by the wayside, and the company operates in a centralized way – that is not necessarily bad in some contexts where the full use of the company's potential with a short-term orientation overcomes the need for flexibility or innovation. But, on the other hand, the absence of any form of bureaucratically inspired direction is not necessarily desirable for the development of a network organization. Thus, we found the difficulties experienced by CFDP and Air Liquide during the suppression of hierarchy altogether relatively reassuring. It is clear that individuals cannot get out from under a hierarchical framework without accompanying support. CFDP's experience shows that it is even difficult to find cohesion through the network when one tries to impose autonomy. Indeed, autonomy cannot be imposed. In addition to this necessary management of the transition, a 'minimal' intervention of the center is always desirable to ensure good functioning of the network. Within the province of the center, one finds the need for fixing the rules of the game to make the network organization possible. These rules concern, on the one hand, the definition of the peripheral unit's field of intervention, and, on the other, the basic rules for the interactions between units.

The center can also intervene to support the implementation of network organization: it then takes on the role of 'setting up the network.' It is clear that if the central management governs all the interactions between peripheral units, one withdraws any possibility of network organization (other than that related to the existence of a 'community of peripheral units,' which is quite clearly a centralized community). This is approximately what happened at Colas where there are few direct relationships, formal or informal, between the peripheral units: all essential information goes through the center and a whole section of the network organization (associated with collaborative projects, transfers of knowledge, or a form of collegiality, partly disappears).

Control by output can also call the network organization into question, particularly if the criteria selected bear upon short-term profitability at the level of each unit. Moderate pressure on the objective of profitability can encourage operations such as exchanges of equipment or personnel, product sales, or the implementation of collaborative projects in the short run. On the other hand, GTIE's case is beyond the upper limit, as the strong pressure existing within the group can induce non-cooperative behavior. Some GTIE companies behave in an opportunistic way with respect to their internal partners, and the interest of a particular company in certain cases tends to override the interests of the group. In addition, a marked pressure on short-term results comes to limit all operations which do not lead to an immediate tangible improvement in profitability in the short run. The strong economic constraint which weighs on the actors can thus limit the possibilities of development of linkages. For a business manager at GTIE: 'Only one thing is important: not to lose money, it's the most important. The desire for strengthening links exists, but it comes afterwards.' The actors in the operational units therefore tend to concentrate on their strategic plan and do not get involved in sharing customers, transferring knowledge or in collegial decision-making.

This marked contradiction between control by output and the network does not mean that one must forget any control in order to make it possible for the network to develop. The tools of control by output preserve all their relevance. These management tools are absolutely necessary for guiding the peripheral units. On the other hand, the uses to which they are put can be much more nuanced: we pass then from tools of control to tools of management. It is thus possible to disseminate in-house information about the performance of units that have a comparable status. This approach of internal benchmarking, tested at Air Liquide, can create a healthy competitiveness. In the same way, one can imagine indicators that correspond to the realization of common goals. Building links at GTIE, forms one of the criteria used to evaluate the peripheral units, but it comes well behind the indicators of performance. The limit is therefore quickly crossed between a hard logic of control by output which destroys the cooperative logic, and the use of tools of control which, by becoming tools of management and internal benchmarking, are by contrast very useful for the development of the network.

The Network and the Clan

In organization by clan, authority exploits values in order to encourage organizational cohesion. What is more, it is sufficient to think of totalitarian regimes or sects to realize fully that adhesion can be incited to the most inhuman systems of values. It is clear that the system of values proposed by the company is in competition with other systems of values to which the individual may adhere: cohesive force is thus limited within a particular organization. The clan can allow an individual to develop a feeling of belonging to the organization − in this sense, it is a mode of organization − but it can also encourage cohesion which uses one of the other three modes of organization. The support of the clan is particularly useful for the network, which implies shared values, as does the clan. This support is expressed in two directions: the creation of a dynamic and the integration and follow-up of individuals. There exists, however, as for the other modes of organization, a major risk for the network if its cohesion depends too much on the clan: paralysis. Table 7.3 summarizes the results concerning combinations of the network and the clan.

Table 7.3 The network and the clan

CLAN	OBJECTIVE OF THE COMBINATION	RISKS	POSSIBLE RESPONSES
Promoting the network	• Creating the dynamism of the network • Avoiding free-riders	• Paralysis by excess	• Reaffirming the objectives associated with the network organization

The clan can be an element of support which is essential for the development of the network. The case of CFDP is a good example of the way in which adhesion to a new type of work relationships and to a new mode of management can be obtained. We have shown the importance of the vision in the progression of the company towards a form of collegial structure. This vision was nothing other than a set of values reaffirmed incessantly by the two leaders of the company in order to create dynamism. It was used as a reference throughout the transformation of the company: all decisions were made with the aim of developing the vision and of diffusing it outside the company. The importance of this type of theme is found in the 'Initiative in the Field' program carried out within Air Liquide. Among the firms studied, Air Liquide is undoubtedly the one which made widest use of the clan, both to generate a feeling of belonging and to encourage the network organization. Organization by clan also plays a significant role in the way in which companies ensure the transmission of values to those who have newly joined. Whether they relate to the integration of values linked to the network or to another type of value, the criteria of recruitment, the mobility of individuals within the company, and the monitoring of careers by the center are very powerful tools. Colas, for example, succeeded in finding a balance thanks to the emphasis placed on the specificity of its activity, at the heart of which autonomy and centralization can easily coexist. This balance is based on the respect of the expertise of central actors who are mainly professionals with experience in the field.

We have already had the opportunity to underline the fact that CFDP found itself confronted with delegates who were free-riding within the group, while at the same time proclaiming an outward attitude of adhesion to the vision. The network organization is particularly vulnerable to this kind of behavior. The clan, by means of the emphasis it places on the vision and values and by playing on socialization, can allow companies to fight against the free-riding phenomenon. It allows a company to stimulate adhesion of its members.

One limit on the recourse to the clan as a complement of the network organization is that of excess, and CFDP provides a good example of this. The internal agents were so worried by the need to carry through the vision that it became the central concern of the company. At certain times in its history, the company found itself unable to make strategic decisions. The emphasis placed on the vision by the mechanisms of the clan had served the network so well that organization by the network had become a paralysing preoccupation for a navel-gazing organization. It thus appears essential not to lose sight of the objectives associated with the network organization: organization by the network should not become an end in itself.

The Combinations of Modes of Organization

The analysis made of the combination of the network with the other modes of organization leads to some more general reflections on organizational cohesion and its overall interpretation, thanks to the concept of the mode of organization. It is necessary first to reflect again on the foundations of organizational cohesion, represented here as a characteristic structured by a significant number of dimensions that we have just started to explore. This concept of organizational cohesion leads us to reflect on the notion of loosely coupled systems. It is therefore appropriate to question the combination of the network with the other modes of organization in a general way, since the preceding development of the discussion has shown the reinforcements or, conversely, the contradictions between the modes of organization.

Organizational cohesion and loosely coupled systems

We began this work with the desire to give body to the concept of the network as a mode of organization. This analysis has led us to distinguish sixteen dimensions which can serve as a basis for organizational cohesion by the network. It is likely that by refining this analysis by studying other company cases, one could multiply the dimensions and obtain an even more detailed understanding of what network organization is. Moreover, we have sketched out the same work for the other modes of organization throughout the discussion of the conceptual framework, but we did not go into the detail of this analysis during the discussion of the cases: this was not the direct object of this research. It is clear that it would be equally possible to distinguish a significant number of dimensions that underlie the three other modes of organization. Each one of these dimensions carries cohesion for the organization. One can thus picture overall cohesion as the result of the cohesion generated by each dimension underlying each of the organizational modes. Each of the four modes of organization thus contributes to organizational cohesion and overall cohesion results from cohesion tied at the same time to the market, to bureaucracy, to the clan, or to the network. In the same way, organizational cohesion related to the network results from the cohesion generated by each of the sixteen dimensions that have been identified. Cohesion of an organization thus seems to be a multidimensional quality resulting from elementary cohesions, which are themselves founded on elementary dimensions.

This concept of organizational cohesion calls for reflection on the concept of loosely coupled system. In our approach, a loosely coupled system is a system with weak cohesion. However, there is always a tendency to associate the strength of the coupling of a system with certain modes of organization. Thus, the network organization would be synonymous with a loosely coupled system, while organization by bureaucracy would ensure that cohesion was strong. Organizational cohesion such as it appears in the four companies studied shows on the contrary that the network can be at the root of strong cohesion, just as much as the other modes of organization. Each organizational mode and even each of the dimensions that underlie it can therefore explain the cohesion of an organization; and the network is no exception. Each mode of organization is called upon, more or less, in any given organization, which leads to overall cohesion for the organization in question which is more or less strong.

Reinforcement or contradiction between the network and other modes of organization

We have just discussed the possibility of combining the organizational modes in order to contribute to organizational cohesion. However, analysis of the combinations of the organizational modes shows clearly that there are both reinforcements and blockages depending on the combination between the various modes of organization. Here, we are interested more particularly in the way in which the other organizational modes can support or threaten organizational cohesion by the network. It seems from the cases studied that cohesion by the network can greatly benefit from the support of the other modes of organization, whether it be the market, the bureaucracy or the clan. However, it appears equally that too great a recourse to the other organizational modes can block cohesion by network. These observations immediately evoke a curve often used in management science: the inverted U-curve. We obviously do not have quantitative data to support this proposal. The only certain point is the general shape of the curve. It is perhaps not exactly an inverted U, it perhaps allows thresholds, it is perhaps more – or less – flat... In any event, its logic is the following: cohesion by the network is reinforced by putting the other modes of organization into effect. However, if their use is excessive, blockages appear which limit the extent of cohesion by the network (see Figure 7.1.). It is also important to note that the shape of this curve necessarily varies over time. We proved, for example, the importance that the clan could have in creating the dynamic needed for evolution towards a network organization. Once this dynamic is launched, promotion of the network approach by the authorities seems less necessary: convergence of values can follow an autonomous course within the framework of the network.

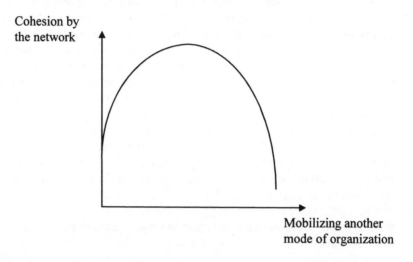

Figure 7.1 Relationship between cohesion by the network and the use of other modes of organization

Conclusion

The objective of this work has been above all to describe a course of development and to draw up a balance sheet after twenty years of network organization. It describes in detail the mechanisms put in place for such network organizations. It shows also that the path is difficult and full of pitfalls. So is the game worth the candle? The many examples collected in our four companies show that on balance they do get their money back. This said, each reader must ask the question of his or her own company. Depending on the key objectives and the context in which a company is developing, it is more, or less, relevant to resort in a more, or less, significant way to network organization.

However, it seems that there are few sectors and activities that can escape network organization. Indeed, we have returned to a time when the environment is more disturbed than that which companies knew during 'the thirty glorious years.'[29] Use of information and communication technologies is still accelerating the process. Companies must be capable of adapting themselves more and more quickly to fluctuating contexts by combining their resources in an original way. The network thus becomes an inevitable way forward. It is also necessary for companies to function at a local base or around clusters of customers, where the autonomy associated with the network is inescapable. Beyond this autonomy, the way in which the network crosses boundaries allows the possibilities of learning and of sharing knowledge to grow. Lastly, evolution towards the democratic company is an even more ambitious project which goes beyond the improvement of economic performance to contribute to changing relationships to work.

Beyond description, we want this work also to provide support for action. It seems important to us now to propose an overall vision which leads to an overall approach for setting up network organization. In our analysis, we have brought out the difficulties associated with transition towards the network. We now regroup these pitfalls in a cross-cutting way; it is essential that they be well identified if one wishes to enter into the transition towards the network in good condition. We shall then emphasise this transition by synthesizing the levers of action which come from observation. In this

29. The period of more than thirty years of growth after World War II.

section, the decision-maker will find a synthetic response to the 'how?' beyond the 'what?' Finally, we will propose an approach to implementation broken up into a series of key steps.

THE PITFALLS OF THE NETWORK

We have shown the pitfalls and the difficulties associated with evolution towards the network bit by bit as we described the mechanisms for it. Here we take them up again, this time in a cross-cutting way, while emphasizing possible solutions.

Blockages at the Level of the Individual

Some problems appear at the level of the individual: the people concerned come across difficulties or refuse to work towards a network organization. One cannot expect a unanimously enthusiastic reception, and, as in any change, some individuals will be more upset than others. It is certain that the network, by the questioning that it entails, gives rise to significant reactions and blockages. Some actors will be more attached than others to traditional hierarchical ways of working and, for them, the transition towards the network will mean real questioning of their rules of behavior.

The first source of blockages is the former 'heads' who lose their status. A senior manager, who becomes an expert or a coordinator within a relatively short space of time, clearly loses a great number of his reference points and prerogatives. Competence and charisma become the only elements on which authority comes to be based. In such a process, those without the necessary expertise find themselves in a difficult situation. This can be interpreted as a healthy process of selection, but also as a difficulty on the level of the whole company. The former 'heads,' whose authority rested primarily on status, are pushed aside, but there are also people who have difficulty finding their place in these new structures although they have precious expertise. Others will hang on to hierarchical ways of working by recreating secret hierarchies in the areas for which they are responsible, which reduces the credibility of the approach as a whole. Companies which want to evolve must be able themselves to fight against such types of behavior. One of the levers that we shall identify in the following section concerns the emphasis on expertise rather than on status. In effect it means giving new points of reference to people for whom ambiguity is difficult to manage. This happens through placing systematic emphasis on themes which bring them together. Support is also an essential element in the success of the transition.

There is also loss of significant points of reference by former subordinates. These have, in effect, been conditioned for many years – notably by an educational system which doesn't always assign a large enough place to initiative – to behave in accordance with a hierarchical model. For them also trauma can be great, and a worker who played his or her role perfectly within a hierarchical framework will not necessarily be able to make good decisions when he or she is given a whole new space for autonomy. Moreover, some of these employees have found their satisfaction outside the company and are not ready to assume new responsibilities within it. Why put up with the stress associated with increased responsibility and the absence of hierarchical points of reference? Autonomy and responsibility are not the elements of reward for everyone, and managers are not excluded from this phenomenon. Support plays a crucial role in this situation as well. It can take place by developing special training intended to make it easier to adopt autonomous ways of behaving. The process must also take into account the development path of pay.

For these two groups of actors, transition can prove to be difficult, and the company can thus be exposed to the risk of free-riders. Faced with developments that they view as unrealistic, counter-productive, and perhaps manipulative, some actors will adopt this type of behavior. It is often easy to pretend to accept the logic of the network while at the same time behaving in contrary ways. This is even more the case as development towards the network is accompanied by the introduction of a margin of maneuver for actors towards whom it is necessary to show trust and leniency. It is therefore important to discover the people who cannot work properly under cross-cutting autonomy as soon as possible. It is bad for the entire company and for the success of the transformation to allow free-riding to develop. Within the framework of setting up the network (see above) the center must mobilize adequate means of support for people who are not completely recalcitrant. On the other hand, this type of project will always be accompanied by resignations. These departures must be managed sufficiently early and in a way which avoids traumatizing the entire organization. Outplacement is a solution well suited to achieving this.

Inter-unit Blockages

As well as the problems of individual adaptation, the history of the company carries a heavy weight in determining the possibility of setting up cross-cutting modes of working. Compartmentalization and pre-existing tensions between departments are also limiting factors. There are also tensions tied to the introduction of autonomy: working across boundaries can be seen as an intrusion into the free space of each unit.

After decades of hierarchical and non-cooperative ways of working, a company approaches the network with the important handicap of a compartmentalized structure. In very compartmentalized groups, each operational unit has developed its own micro-culture within the group, a micro-culture suited to a particular environment. In some of the units studied, the sphere of reference was firstly the operational unit, then the group. This isolation within a local area is even more marked when the units carry different names. In the case of units that are very closed and even in opposition to each other, the work of setting up the network falls above all on the central unit. It is thus important to assure the transition by taking incremental steps (see above) which put the emphasis above all on the most concrete projects, projects that will have impact in the short term.

These progressive steps are also suited to the situations often found where the peripheral units operate with a significant amount of autonomy. The fact of wanting to develop cross-cutting links can often be viewed as a direct intrusion into their field of autonomy. The 'not invented here' syndrome is very widespread in groups where autonomy chimes with compartment-talization. This results in experiments carried out in parallel in several units. Any attempt to transpose a solution coming from another unit is then perceived as a failure, and it is clearly difficult to evolve towards collective learning and the sharing of knowledge in such a context. The difficulty is even greater when an attempt is made to propose to the customer base of one unit some services provided by another unit in another field. The more that customers are seen as the property of a unit's actors, the more important becomes the impression of intrusion into its reserved domain. In such a situation, it is necessary to think again in terms of how to guide the change and of what progressive steps will be the most appropriate.

The Failure of the Network Dynamic

Evolution towards the network rests on a fragile process which must both lead to a real change in state of mind and base itself upon this change. This process is itself in part emergent and thus requires many interactions that are not always easy to develop.

The cooperative approach is written into a long-term process in which trust is essential. The first brake on cooperation is almost certainly the workers' orientation towards time, which does not encourage them to sign up to a perspective of long-term exchange. Submerged by daily work in the field, they have difficulty in accepting a human investment that they perceive to have uncertain outcomes. They will put even less of themselves into it if they perceive the cooperation as risky, if for example they have to provide one of their contacts: they would then be afraid of losing a customer because of the intervention of another unit. The links must therefore be woven step by step between the actors at the periphery. But these links are necessarily fragile in the period of change. It is thus essential to take special care about the division of roles and revenues in joint projects. These safeguards are just as necessary to preserve the future network of relationships as within the framework of inter-company relations. If they are not put in place, future cooperation runs a strong risk of becoming endangered.

For the network dynamic to take off, the actors must come into contact with each other. Every missed opportunity for cross-cutting work or learning serves to delay the development of the network. Information about the resources, competences and interests of the other members of the organization is precious for the development of the network. The center has an important role to play in limiting the number of these missed opportunities. It must ensure that the network is set up but without going too far in the opposite direction. Indeed, it is not a solution to regulate the way in which exchanges between units take place. It is impossible to force the actors in an organization to weave autonomous links. If the network dynamics are to work well and to work in the long term, it is also necessary that individuals create links of affinity with each other. The interpersonal relationship is essential, and mutual appreciation cannot be forced. If the center wants to force the dynamic processes of the network, this is a dangerous and unrealistic inclination. It is thus necessary to navigate very carefully between two reefs: missed opportunities and over-regulation.

THE LEVERS OF ACTION

The path to the network, even if it is attractive and praised by the consultant-muses, nonetheless stays littered with pitfalls. It was important to analyze these pitfalls and the preceding paragraphs have rehearsed them. Let us now look further at the ways in which action is supported and specify the principal levers that the manager can use.

The Focus Points

In a process of change that mobilizes autonomous units to a significant extent, it is essential to lay down a certain number of markers, points to which the members of an organization, necessarily disoriented, can attach themselves, points of focusing. These focus points are more than simple federating themes or a vision of the organization, they are at the heart of the process of change. They make it possible for the members of the organization to find their place again and for the organization to structure itself. There are at least two themes which can play this part in the current sociocultural and competitive context: relationships with customers, and expertise.

The relationship with customers is a fashionable topic, which does not mean that it is no use as a focal point, quite the contrary. First of all, the customer relationship makes it possible to legitimate internally the progress towards more autonomy. It can equally assure progress towards cutting across boundaries to serve the customer. In any case, this theme of customer relationships serves as a guide for individuals who can no longer turn to central management to solve their problems and who lose their reference points in a situation of autonomy. All variants are possible in the degree of reciprocal involvement in the relationship with customers, but the most interesting variant is certainly the development towards external control by the customer. This occurs naturally in some sectors, such as that of the building sector, but it can be extended to other fields as shown in the CFDP experiment. The message would be: 'put the customer in charge.' It is interesting to note that in many cases, customers are ready to involve themselves in the internal processes of their suppliers and, in any event, to share ideas with them.

A second essential focal point is that of expertise. The transition towards a network structure involves, as we have emphasized, the loss of reference points for former 'heads' as well as for former 'subordinates.' This transition must not be carried out at the expense of devaluing competence usually held by the majority of actors who see their hierarchical status called into question. To avoid this, emphasis must be placed on valuing the knowledge of these experts. The richness of the knowledge held at various levels of the organization must be stressed. The message to the experts is therefore simple: it is better for them to be sought out spontaneously for their expertise than to intervene in command mode because of their status in the hierarchy. It thus becomes essential to emphasize local expertise, and information and communication technologies are an ideal support for making each person's experience known.

The Credibility of the Approach

It is up to the managers at various levels to make this approach credible. Indeed, in an organization where the logics of bureaucracy and market were dominant, it is tempting to consider emphasis on the network as a passing fashion, or even as an attempt at manipulation by the center. The habits of hierarchical behavior and compartmentalization die hard.

Management indicators must allow workers to become involved in setting up the network and to be accountable for it. The contradictions between network, market and bureaucracy can be strong. The dictatorship of results-by-unit reinforces compartmentalization and does not encourage the kind of altruism necessary to a relationship of trust. If market mechanisms are added to these evaluation criteria for regulating the relationships between units, an even more important risk is run. It is thus essential to introduce the means and rewards needed to develop autonomous and cross-boundary relationships into the budgetary and planning processes. Cross-boundary working must be as much a part of the strategic objectives as of the operational ones. The simple fact of introducing a section devoted to network operations within a strategic plan can be an important factor. It is also necessary to allocate the means necessary for these operations: tools for information sharing, budgets, and especially the freedom to use time for dialogue between units. Time must be invested outside the logic of immediate profitability. In terms of management, it necessarily implies arbitrage between short-term profitability (and thus maximization of the time spent on the unit's operational problems) and long-term investment in the network relationships.

It is crucial, beyond the formal mechanisms of the plan and the budget, to give the organizational actors some stake to make the proceedings credible. If, for example, a company wants to encourage relationships with customers, it is important that the units in contact in an industrial group enjoy a status equivalent to that of industrial or operational management. The actors in the field need to be appreciated. In the same way, it is necessary to offer opportunities for career advancement to those with expertise and competence, even if these opportunities follow a different path from the hierarchical ladder. These stakes can also take the form of guarantees in respect of past hierarchical accomplishments. The center must fight constantly against the return of compartmentalization and undesirable hierarchical relationships. It is even sometimes necessary to go further and offer actual guarantees to the periphery. One possible solution is to entrust cross-unit coordination to actors who are seen to belong to the periphery. In order to guarantee the process, individuals from the ranks, rather than those from central bodies, are chosen. The legitimacy of coordinators is an essential point. It is undoubtedly necessary to accept, or even require, some resignations in order better to embed the network.

Implementing the Network

The reader will have understood that the center must be the engine and the guarantor of a dynamic process that must then find how to develop autonomously. The center must first of all support members of the organization during the transitional phase and must also stimulate cross-cutting projects and links systematically.

As well as factors tied to the incentive mechanisms which are necessary to entice a hierarchical organization to start a dynamic process, support is an important aspect of the center's role. As has been indicated, the actors in an organization can be recalcitrant or simply skeptical about setting up a network. It is thus possible to provide specific training for each type of responsibility, that can help actors to learn to be autonomous. The peripheral actors must also learn how to use local networks of competence which belong to other units or to their immediate environment – customers, suppliers – to find solutions to the problems that they meet. It is up to the center to stimulate setting up various forms of communities, and specially communities of practices which allow knowledge to be shared between actors with common concerns. The solution of mentoring young recruits by more established members can help integration into the organization. This system can be extended to other groups already found in the organization. The former 'heads' necessarily feel a need for the recognition that they can find in a dialogue with central actors, but for some of them external intervention may prove to be necessary and coaching then seems to be a suitable method.

The center is moreover irreplaceable in its role of setting up the network. This important role is obviously part of the transitional phase, but also of the organization's operations thereafter. The central actors can use their unique knowledge of the organization to stimulate the meetings and exchanges that will lead to concrete projects or communities of practice. It is particularly difficult to go from a status where one is the key actor in mediation between units to that of simple go-between. This requires constant discipline, in particular to accept encouraging the setting up of the network where control is concerned. If one wants communities of practice to emerge, it is necessary to get away from the desire to control output systematically. Central actors must trust their members to produce rewarding results in the long term, which can then be disseminated to the whole organization. Following the same line of thought, a central manager told us that he forced himself systematically, when he knew the solution to a problem posed by one peripheral actor, to redirect him towards another peripheral actor rather than give him the solution directly. It is such practices that make it possible to clear the way for real cooperation between the units.

PUTTING THE NETWORK TO WORK

This final section sets out a general approach for transition towards the network. The first phase is that of organizational diagnosis. It helps an organization to evaluate its current situation and to define what balance it seeks between the different modes of organization. Then comes the identification of the brakes and levers that can be expected in that current situation, and then the choice of route towards the goal.

The Organizational Diagnosis

The organizational diagnosis can be based directly on the conceptual framework which was defined in the first chapter of this book. Then we can add the results of our work on the network organization to this diagnosis. The primary objective of the diagnosis must be to assess the organization's current situation: what is the contribution of each organizational logic to the cohesion of the whole? The analytical grid presented on page 156 is a first guide for this diagnostic work. Where bureaucratic influence is concerned, it is essential to find out the respective importance of control by input and control by output. Control by output indeed leaves more room for autonomy, whereas control by input limits the margin of maneuver for the actors. The path towards the network can therefore differ according to the bureaucratic mechanisms which are used. The clan is a crucial factor in the diagnosis. It is indeed by thinking about clan mechanisms in action that one can find future vectors of cohesion which will help to support the development of the network. It is also essential to know the organization's capacity to use its culture to support the transition. As far as the market is concerned, two principal types of mechanisms can be at work: putting units into internal and external competition and using price systems in internal transactions. Finally, it is important to determine to what extent the organization is or is not based upon network mechanisms, as well as the degree of formalization or of secrecy of these networks.

Once the analysis of the mechanisms underlying the current cohesion of the organization has taken place, it is appropriate to raise the question of the evolution desired. It is obvious that the questioning must take strategic aspects into account at this stage. Chapter 3 set out some of the advantages of developing an increased degree of autonomy, while the goals of working across boundaries were presented in chapters 4 and 5. Two types of questions must be answered before initiating evolution towards the network. The first concerns the degree of cohesion which is desired. The second concerns the contribution of each mode of organization, particularly the network, to the new configuration.

Identifying Restraints and Key Levers

The position at the outset determines what the issues are that can arise during evolution towards the network, but also what are the levers to be used. Two cases seem characteristic of candidates for setting up networks: the case of the bureaucratic company and that of the market company.

In the first case, organizational cohesion is based above all on mechanisms of control by input. The transformation to be envisaged is thus two-fold: at the same time it is necessary to introduce autonomy and to encourage cross-boundary operations. It is to be expected that various 'blocking' syndromes, as described above, will appear: individual mental blockages, inter-unit deadlocks, and risks of checks to the progress in changing relationships. Compartmentalization and inability to function outside hierarchical points of reference are the rule in this type of organization. But paradoxically, the absence of autonomy can prove to be a trump card, if a radical approach (see above) can be put to work. Indeed, it was noted that in bureaucratic organizations, there was often a secret network operation. The actors are quick to play around with the rules when these are deemed unsuitable. It is thus possible that these underground logics can be used to support the setting up of the network.

Market companies result from the desire to introduce decentralization. Many companies have gone from a bureaucratic logic to an operation that is largely based on an organization made up of profit centers which combine the price mechanism and control by output. In this type of organization, autonomy is acquired at all levels, but the transition towards the network is no less difficult. If, in the name of market principles, competition or rivalry in the distribution of financial flows is introduced into the relations between units, compartmentalization can become particularly well established. The situation is then even more difficult than in bureaucratic companies: the members of the operational units do not necessarily ignore each other, but on the other hand they may hate each other. In addition, the setting up of the network can be seen as intrusion into the reserved territory of autonomous units, that is to say, as calling their autonomy into question. The network cannot be imposed; in this type of situation it is an incremental approach which seems the best adapted.

Possible Courses to Take

We propose two possible paths for moving towards an increasing role for network logic in producing organizational cohesion. These two routes flow directly from a company's situation at the outset, and therefore from the restraints and levers identified in the diagnosis. They correspond to the two frequently-met but delicate situations for large companies that we identified above. It is clear that companies that are less Manichean in their approach will experience an easier transition.

The first possible scenario is that of the bureaucratic company whose cohesion rests primarily on mechanisms of control by input. It is clear that in such a situation the only possible approach necessarily includes an important deliberate strand. The use of hierarchical power is discretionary, and only the center is capable of breaking the hierarchical mold. Only a major reorganization, including modification of the organization charts and a reduction in the number of hierarchical levels, can allow transition to take place. In this type of development, the center plays an essential role in supporting the network and putting it into place. It can draw especially on the secret networks hidden within the former bureaucratic structure. The emerging dynamics can then pick up the baton, but such a revolution is always long and difficult.

The other scenario is that of the market company, in which market mechanisms and control by output were able to generate rivalry and tension between the units. In such a situation, the transition towards the network can prove to be delicate. Two principal processes can be mobilized: an incremental approach initiated by the center, and capitalizing on entrepreneurship. These two mechanisms can be combined. The center can first intervene in an incremental manner by stimulating the development of cross-boundary experience within the network, by favoring the development of links, and by coordinating activities. Plans linked to cross-cutting management of knowledge are in line with this perspective. The stimulation of local innovation and initiative can generate a real dynamic of entrepreurship: the actors on the periphery can become true bearers of cross-boundary dynamics. The center must then serve as an intermediary and nurture these champions of innovation. If the richness of autonomy can be transformed into cooperative leaps thanks to the carriers of cross-boundary projects, the gamble of the network is already won.

Appendix I
Presentation of the companies

The research presented in this work is based on the in-depth analysis of the situation of four companies. This appendix gives the reader the principal elements about their organization, their strategy, and the context in which they evolve. The structures described are as when the research was done; by the time of the publication of the research, some changes might have occurred. The main figures have been updated.

AIR LIQUIDE

Air Liquide completely reorganized its operation around small-sized units which had strong autonomy, with horizontal structures and that were also interconnected. There are three main types of peripheral structures: service providers for a given country, national production establishments, and customer service centers that carry out production on a local basis. Thus there is both geographical and vertical specialization within the group. The case makes a detailed study of a national establishment and a region (or customer service center).

The Company

Air Liquide is the world leader in the production and the distribution of air gases (oxygen, hydrogen, CO_2, rare gases, etc). The company makes 72% of its turnover through the sale of industrial gas, while the health sector (medical gases) accounts for 17% and clients in electronics correspond to 11%. The group is strongly internationalized, with Europe's part in the turnover being 55% while America accounts for 30%, Asia/Pacific 13% and Africa 2%. The number of people working for the group's companies is 30800, the turnover 7.9 billion Euros for a result of 7 billion Euros.

Principal Strategic Elements

Air Liquide was created to exploit a technique that allows the separation of the components of air. It is on the basis of constantly renewed technological advances in this field and their applications that the company developed. If other gases were added to the principal components of air, diversification concerns only the applications and the materials necessary to the utilization of gases produced by the company. Air Liquide masters the techniques of production, distribution, and the utilization of air gases. The control of these techniques requires constant innovation in order to find new fields of application and solutions for sectors in constant evolution.

The development strategy of the company evolves both via the discovery of new applications, if possible with strong value added and by way of a growing internationalization of its activity. Growth is primarily internal. Air Liquide's strategy consists in controlling a technological core, which is constantly being modified to allow new customized applications.

The Company's Structure

Air Liquide is organized in subsidiary companies for the various countries where the company is established. These subsidiaries are directly attached to the headquarters and the structure within each subsidiary is similar, though more or less developed depending on the size of the corresponding market

Air Liquide's industrial trade can be broken down into three large activities that one can find in each subsidiary company: pipeline gas, engineering, and commercial trade. Each activity is also dependent on the headquarters. The pipeline division produces gases in large volume in installations on a national scale (or even worldwide for certain gases). This activity directly provides gases via pipelines to a certain number of important clients. It also provides the raw materials necessary to commercial trade. Engineering is both a service provider for the pipeline division for whom it designs installations, for commercial trade to which it provides installations intended to produce directly at the client's site, and for direct clients, for whom it designs large-scale installations. Commercial trade – industrial gases and services – is what directly interests us in this case study. It consists in selling to regional clients of gas in bulk (large volumes delivered in liquid form by truck), in tanks, or produced on site at the client's plant. The health field also constitutes a distinct entity, with the required gases, the degree of purity, and the distribution systems all being very different.

There are also group projects that are always directly attached to the headquarters. These projects relate to the fields considered to be strategic for the development of the company. They are structures of coordination in which managers do not have hierarchical bonds with the subsidiary companies. These global structures of coordination have one person in charge by country and must sell their products or activities to the regional managers.

In addition to operational management, a certain number of staff managements exist with the central headquarters: technology management, health-group management, research and marketing management, legal management, financial management, management of safety and human resources strategy. Figure A.1, represents a simplified flow chart of Air Liquide on the group level.

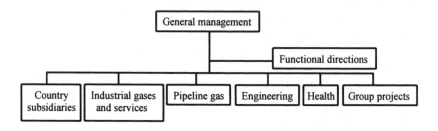

Figure A.1 Simplified organizational chart of Air Liquide at the group level

Study of this case relates to commercial trade in France, the corresponding structure is the Industrial Gases and Services department, directly linked to the headquarters. It is indeed this department which is the pioneer in matters of organization at Air Liquide. It is in commercial trade that organizational innovations were initially made in the group, other trades being in the course of transformation. One finds the same evolution for this trade in the countries where Air Liquide is present.

The current structure of the Industrial Gases and Services department results from a reform of the structures introduced in 1992. The goal of this reform was to install an 'organization of small teams devoted to a market, an area, or a field of competence'. This new structure centers around regions (33 in France and 200 in the world). It allows for 'taking into account needs in service to the client ... [and] ... favors the initiative and autonomy of each member of personnel.' The reform was launched under the name of 'Initiative in the Field'.

The department is organized by various sub-units, certain ones having the status of management; others are peripheral units (Figure A.2). There are five central functional units whose directors are members of the department's management committee: sales management, IT management, human resources management, industrial management, and development and services management. The persons in charge of security and quality do not

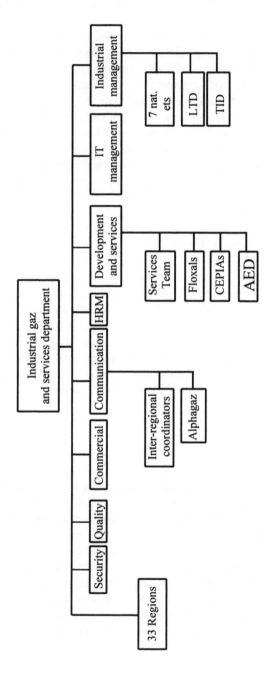

Figure A.2 Industrial Gases and Services Flow Chart

have the status of directors; they nevertheless manage central processing units.

In addition to the regions and the national establishments, there are a certain number of units that are dependent on the industrial gases and services department but these have a status of peripheral units. Some of these are internal suppliers of gas or equipment: Logistic and Transport Department (LTD), Application and Equipment Department (AED), and Technical and Installations Department (TID). Other units are those of support that provide a certain number of services to the regions. The Centers of Expertise in Processes, Installations and Applications (CEPIA), the two Floxal Teams, and the Service Team are the principal units of support; their role is presented in the parts of this work that discuss them. Alphagaz, a subsidiary company specialized in special gases, is dependent on commercial management, as are some inter-regional coordinators.

Structure of the Peripheral Units

Two peripheral units were the subject of a particularly detailed study: the production establishments and the regions. The other units mentioned above are national support teams which include a reduced number of experts. The regions constitute the core of commercial trade. The Industrial Gases and Services regions comprise between 20 and 70 people. The structure resulting from the reform of 1992 is a 'flat' structure, the regional manager being the only actor to have a hierarchical bond with the whole of the personnel of the region. There are a certain number "experts" or "guarantors," but they have no hierarchical role.

The structure of the national establishments varies according to the activities handled by each establishment. There are in fact seven establishments which ensure the conditioning of some gases that would not be profitable if done regionally. The establishments also take care of other activities like the maintenance or the testing of tanks. The structure of the establishment that we have studied in detail includes several hierarchical levels but one finds the same concern about autonomy as that existing in the regions. Certain people are linked directly to the person in charge of the establishment without having any direct subordinates.

The establishment studied has two principal activities: the retesting of tanks/bottles (testing and maintenance of the tanks/bottles) and production of certain gases. A manager is at the head of each one of these activities, having a hierarchical role. Each activity is then divided into small teams. Some of these teams are coordinated by a manager (a products and services team or production line team for example), others are autonomous (like the park team or maintenance).

Analysis of the Context

The context in which Air Liquide has been growing is characterized by the association of a need for autonomy and a certain integration of activity. The essential motivation behind the reform of 1992 is the improvement of the service brought to the customer. Increased competition in the air gases sector made necessary a new approach concerning clients. As we have seen, the structure of Air Liquide is complex. The old structure forced the clients to deal with several interlocutors in order to satisfy their various needs. The new structure gives a smaller team the capacity to make decisions and the possibility of knowing the client better. The units thus choose according to their knowledge of the region, the axes of development best adapted to their clientele. A point of equal importance is that of the speed of intervention on the client's plant: effective intervention requires a preliminary knowledge of the details of plants.

In the same spirit, part of the activity of the regions includes the installation at the client's premises of the storage or the on-site gas production units (Floxal). For this activity it is necessary to be able to set up a project that is adapted to the client's requirements, being able to constantly evolve with the times. Development thus occurs through continual presence in the field which alone can make it possible to detect new needs and thus to develop new projects.

Air Liquide's evolution strategy includes the will to develop the services associated with gas. This capacity to ensure all of the services associated with the sale of gas constitutes one of the group's distinct competences. If one reconsiders the example of installations at the client's plant, the gas is brought to the heart of the production tool/machine of the client. Air Liquide takes on the entire service and, in addition to installation, ensures on-site maintenance.

If it thus seems necessary to leave the regions a large margin of maneuver, activity of the group also requires a marked integration in several other fields.

Since the creation of Air Liquide, innovation constitutes the key to the development of the company. This work concerns all aspects of the trade from the design of factories to small gas manufacturing units and from containers that allow gas storage to searching for new materials or fields of application. Research and development are carried out on a global scale and the efforts necessary for this greatly exceed the resources of a simple regional unit. Specific developments can be carried out in regions only insofar as the regions have the support of all of the structures.

In searching for increased autonomy, Air Liquide chose to de-localize towards the regions for the conditioning (bottling) of certain gases. However, the economic constraints are such that the national establishments were maintained for conditioning other gases. Moreover, the Industrial Gases and Services department buys air gases from the Pipeline department. For the gas production to be competitive, it must be done in large factories, which themselves are supplied directly by important clients. For certain gases, there are only a few sites of production per country, for others (helium for example), global production is done by only three sites. The minimal scale production in the gas trade thus involves production that goes well beyond a region's consumption.

As we have stated, the needs/requirements of the client are constantly changing little by little as they modify their production and as new needs appear. The installations and the size of storage tanks must frequently be modified. The company must thus always have all types of installations available to them and manage flows of equipment between the regions. It is certain that the cost of such flexibility would be prohibitory at the regional level, but flows are compensated for at the national level. The management of the equipment stock is thus perceived at Air Liquide as having to be centralized. The same goes for the bottle/tank stock whose maintenance is also handled centrally.

CFDP

CFDP is an insurance company specializing in legal protection; it is the French leader in its activity. Its products, for the most part, are intended for private individuals to whom it provides, for a fee, assistance in the event of litigation and financing of lawyers in the event of a lawsuit. Certain products are also developed for artisan craftsmen or very small companies. Its direct customers are insurance intermediaries (2000 brokers or agents[30]) who handle the distribution of insurance contracts to private individuals. The company is, however, in contact with the final client for the handling of litigations. Unlike to other insurance companies, CFDP does not have a network of exclusive agents. The company as a whole is comprised of about a hundred employees, or delegates, for whole of France.

In 1991, the company became associated with AGF, a major French insurance company, to create a subsidiary company with equal shares: Protexia. After the failure of their own legal protection company, AGF decided to resort to CFDP to take over running this activity. Protexia in fact

30. Brokers are the representatives of their clients and seek for them the best insurance offer there is in order to meet a definite need. Agents represent a principal company whose products they distribute; they generally have exclusivity on a given territory. There are also intermediaries having a mixed broker-agent status.

is completely managed by CFDP representatives. Protexia accounted for approximately 50% of the turnover in 1996.

The company's capital was held by its two creators/former directors and by the investment companies SDR and the SIPAREX. In 1992, the two directors announced their intention of leaving the capital and the leadership of the company, in the middle term. In 1995, the institutional investors did the same thing within a span of one or two years. This led to a project where the delegates and the intermediary insurance partners bought out the company. This was seen as the ultimate stage of CFDP's project. The buyout went successfully since approximately a quarter of the capital was held by the representatives and the other three quarters by the intermediary partners. However, AGF demanded that they be the major shareholder in Protexia's activity, which in turn introduced a major shareholder for this activity. Current operation is maintained both for Protexia's activity and that of CFDP, but the rise in power of AGF is clearly a risk to the future of the CFDP 'project'.

Principal Strategic Elements

The company not having exclusive network agents, it must convince the brokers and agents of other companies to work with it for legal protection. However, during the 1980s the majority of insurance companies created their own legal protection company, thus beginning to compete directly with CFDP. The insurance agents in turn underwent strong pressure to accept the products of their company and the brokers saw the offer expand. One can well understand how only a significant differentiation could make it possible for the company to survive and to continue developing after the middle of the 1980s. This differentiation went first through a very broad pallet of services offered to the insurance intermediaries. We will see that the partnership with the latter goes well beyond a simple client-supplier relationship. This approach, using the relations with the insurance intermediaries, finds its complementary justification in the increased competition exerted by mutual insurance companies. In effect, the mutual insurance companies distribute their product directly, without agents or brokers. However, they develop quickly (they represent now more than 50% of the market of private individuals) thus threatening the survival of CFDP's direct customers. It is thus vital for the company to help the intermediaries improve their offer and to remain competitive.

Another key element of CFDP's strategy is a new approach in the world of insurance: the contracts they propose are no longer standard contracts. The representatives draft custom contracts with the intermediaries. Furthermore, there is no control over the operations carried out by the intermediaries. This approach breaks with the old role of traditional 'inspectors' sent by the conventional insurance companies and has attracted a significant number of agents.

Structure of the Company

The current structure (see Figure A.3) was put into place in 1996. It is based on a gathering together into teams of the delegates who are representatives of the company for a given geographical region. The aim of the central structure, characterized by democratic operation, is to allow for representation of all of the teams, the evolution towards collective decision-making and transmission of information between the delegations. One characteristic of the company is linking a customer (insurance intermediary) with each representative during the team meetings and higher-level meetings. Thus, certain partner clients can take part in all decisions concerning general interest.

The teams are grouped into six regions. Each one names a twin pair (representative and intermediary) representing the team at the regional committee; each area is then represented by a twin pair in the Inter-Regional Committee (IRC) which thus is composed of twelve people. The two company founders – always shareholders and former general managers – can possibly attend the meetings of the IRC, but not necessarily: they do not form a part of the committee. On the other hand, the Ethics and Orientation Committee (EOC) is composed of the two former leaders and some of the former members of the IRC. It is the IRC that made it possible to launch the buyout project carried out by the delegates and insurance intermediaries. This buyout project marked the achievement of the vision of the company's founders.

Analysis of the Context

It has been said that all of CFDP's strategy is founded on the development of privileged relationships with the insurance intermediaries. The delegates must be present and able to quickly make the decisions necessary to meet the intermediaries' expectations. One of the keys to CFDP's success lies in the quality of the dialogue and the projects which come about between intermediaries and delegates. For this dialogue to be initiated, it is essential that the representative be considered responsible, autonomous and capable of accompanying the intermediary in his development. Only autonomy paves the way for capacity of adaptation in the insurance world.

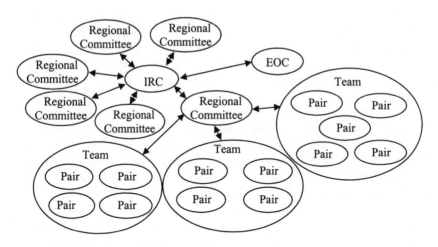

Figure A.3 The current structure of CFDP

Meeting the agents' expectations means innovation. This innovation means as much the services proposed to the insurance intermediaries as contracts themselves. In both cases, an adapted solution can only be developed along with the agent and according to his individual needs. This implies that the delegate can himself define the contracts he proposes to the intermediary and that he has the possibility of engaging himself. The fact that the delegates are responsible mediators or intermediaries who can act without systematically having to ask for the company's approval is greatly appreciated by the agents. Of course, traditional companies use standard contracts more as with 'products' it is difficult to make modifications. If an intermediary wishes to modify a contract, he must 'sell' this modification to his client and also convince the company's central department of the value of this modification.

However, a certain number of the internal organization's elements can only be dealt with at a global level (e.g. the problems of structure and organization or rather elements concerning the overall strategy). The representatives' and intermediaries' drawing up of the buyout project could not have been done at the delegation or team level. The same applies to making a certain number of decisions concerning functional support, choosing of an accounting software program, or even adopting an intranet system.

In the same way, relations with certain external agents sometimes require an interlocutor to speak in the name of the whole company. This is especially true in the case of the relationship with AGF within the framework of Protexia. The existence of a central mediator is necessary in order to envisage an agreement with another insurance group. The relationships with certain public organizations, such as the national insurance commission must also be managed globally.

COLAS

Colas is the world leader in road construction with a turnover of 7.6 billion Euros for a result of 113 million Euros in 2002. Its workforce comprises 55800 people. Road construction activity accounts for 69% of its turnover, to which can be added 13% for sales of materials and products, and 3% for safety, signs and signals. Civil engineering, pipes, and electricity account for 7% of activity, building construction only 3%, and railway projects 1%. The geographical distribution of the turnover is as follows: 55.3% in metropolitan France, 3.3% in French overseas administrative departments and territories (DOM-TOM), 14.0% in Europe, 5.1% for the Indian-Asia/Africa-Oceanic zone, and finally 22.3% for the Americas zone.

The principal shareholder is Bouygues (95.36%). Bouygues therefore has a large majority. Nevertheless, as the major shareholder it appears that Bouygues seldom intervenes in the running of Colas. Bouygues' influence essentially comes down to delineating Colas' activities and selecting the dividends policy. Any potential diversifications in Colas' activity must follow an interconnected logic of diversification. In addition, the dividend distribution policy determines the capacities of investment.

However, occasional deals have resulted from the influence of Bouygues: the takeover of Sacer in 1992 and then of Screg under the same conditions in 1996. Sacer and Screg were two entities of the Bouygues group, and were more integrated into it. These deals fit well into the framework of Colas' strategy of which one of the major axes is the consolidation of its position within French territory: it was therefore a good opportunity for Colas. The decision was by no means imposed upon the group.

Principal Strategic Elements

The group's strategy is based on its fundamental activity: the construction of roads. This activity also includes any intervention on any surface requiring the use of road resurfacing: parking lots, private roads, airplane runways, etc. The few diversifications carried out within the framework of this strategy follow a connected logic of diversification. The principal subsidiaries of diversification also intervene in the following fields: safety installations (Somaro), roadsigns and markings (Ses), distribution networks (Spac), traffic regulation systems (Siat), or the use of highways (Cofiroute).

The company's development is consequently going through a reinforcement of the activity in France, which is associated with geographical diversification. In both cases, the growth is primarily an external growth. In France, this is due to the fragility of the balance of competition, which, because of the very weak growth of the volume of business dealt with, is likely to be upset as soon as a competitor increases its market share to the detriment of the others. Internationally, the intimate knowledge of the specificity of local conditions involves a buyout.

General Structure

The organization chart of the group includes a certain number of operational departments and functional departments which report directly to general management. The functional departments are as follows: legal, finance, organization-accounting, communication, equipment, information technologies, audit, human resources, and finally research and development.

The operational departments break down into seven regional subsidiaries for France: Southwest, North-Picardy, Midi-Mediterranean, Center-West, East, Ile de France/Normandy and the Rhône-Alps. To the seven presidents of the regional subsidiary companies can be added two general managers who are responsible for the larger world zones (International West and International East). Sacer and Screg, as well as the subsidiary companies corresponding to the activities of diversification (Somaro, Ses, Spac, Siat, Cofiroute), are also directly under the general management. They make up independent sub-groups as far as the principal strategic variables are concerned. As for Sacer and Screg, the logic of the group here is only to obtain a greater market share with two distinct brands. The case study is thus limited to the heart of the group, that is to say to the entities carrying the Colas label.

The principle which governs the relations between the headquarters and the subsidiary companies is that of autonomy, which we will later find in the periphery. This principle of autonomy was confirmed at the time of the 'subsidiarization' in 1983. The general management and, more specifically, the president of the group nevertheless maintain an unquestionable power of injunction in all aspects that touch on the development of the group as a whole and with the allowance of resources. The functional departments primarily have a role of counsel and do not have a direct hierarchical link with their counterparts in the subsidiary companies. Informal interactions are very frequent between the subsidiary companies and the headquarters. In addition, there is a certain compartmentalization between the regional subsidiary companies, whether it be in the relations between subsidiary chairmen or functional departments. Contact is rather infrequent, apart from the semi-annual national meetings organized by the head office.

Each regional subsidiary company has a staff made up of the following departments: information technologies, accounting, technique (laboratory of control), legal, human resources, communication and equipment. The peripheral units report directly to the regional subsidiary company, which is a structure of coordination and animation. There are 1200 such units worldwide. The peripheral units can be agencies (in general cases) or sub-subsidiary companies. The sub-subsidiary companies are the result of operations of external growth and can operate under a brand different from the Colas brand, always from the perspective of increasing marketshare.

Structure of the Peripheral Units

It is therefore the agency which constitutes the basic peripheral unit. The agencies (or centers or sub-subsidiaries in certain cases) are the basic establishments which make up the Colas network. In France, there are 120 establishments of this type. It is at this lowest level where a strategy of competitiveness is determined. The agencies' field of action is equivalent to a department. This field of action therefore corresponds to the divisions of the Departmental Office of Equipment (Direction Départementale de l'Equipement), an administrative public department which plays a significant role within the framework of public construction sites. In certain cases, a Unit for Major Works can be added to the agencies in order to ensure coordination and provide the supervisory staff necessary for large construction sites. Large construction sites constitute a different trade altogether and represent only a small share of activity. This unit does not have its own means (it has only three people), but it uses the equipment of the agencies operating in the sectors where it intervenes.

The case study focuses on two of these agencies. In both cases, the same type of internal structure can be found (Figure A.4). The head of the agency is the director of the company: he or she can be assisted (or not) by an operating manager who deals more specifically with the aspects of construction sites.

The operational component is handled by sector managers who coordinate all of the construction sites for a given zone. The construction site managers are responsible for a construction site on which they lead a team of workers. The construction site managers are under the responsibility of a sector manager, which means that they generally operate in a particular zone. Nevertheless, this assigned post is not final, and it can be modified according to the activity in the various sectors.

The agencies also include a certain number of functional staff (which corresponds to a portion of the departments found in the subsidiary companies or headquarters. The administrative manager has under his responsibility a customer accountant, a supplier accountant, a personnel manager, and, in certain cases, an accountant for production units (production of raw materials). There is also a design office made up of two or three people. The design office works out the technical aspects of projects in order to respond to invitations to tender. A person from the subsidiary company's laboratory is also present within the agency in order to carry out the controls necessary for quality follow-up. The workshop manager handles the maintenance and distribution of the agency's machines and has a team of mechanics. The dispatcher is responsible for the optimization of the use of the field-installed machines.

Production units are also under the control of the agencies. These units are frequently acquired in a joint venture with competitors because of the considerable size of the investments necessary. Three types of units exist: production of 'white' materials (roadway constitution), stations of coating (road coating), and factories of emulsion (mixture of water and bitumen).

Figure A.4 Internal Structure of Colas' Agencies

Analysis of the Context

One of the major principles of the Colas organization is decentralization. Therefore, the annual report of the board of directors reads: 'the organization of the group, made up of flexible and decentralized structures, profit centers of human size, makes it possible to combine creative autonomy and strong identities, within the framework of a group policy and a common project of development.' It is this approach which held our attention during the selection of the case. It fulfills the demands of the road construction field, and the actors justify the decentralization of structures by a certain number of contextual elements. Nevertheless, a strong integration is also necessary to satisfy other constraints.

The unit of reference in the road construction field is the construction site. It therefore concerns a project, and each project is different from the preceding one and mobilizes the know-how of the group in a particular way. The work is thus necessarily custom-made, and numerous adaptations are required.

In addition, construction sites in France are of a small size. Indeed, France is a country whose road network is very developed. There are not a lot of large construction sites, such as those which can be found in Third World countries. Construction sites in general have a maximum duration of two weeks for an average amount of 50 000 Euros. Even when a contract of a significant amount is obtained, it can be for the maintenance of an entire network of a local community and break down into a series of mini-construction sites ranging from the construction of one roundabout to the repair of a municipal schoolyard. Large construction sites could be centralized, but the activity, such as it arises in France, means leaving a large initiative in the field in order to respond to particular expectations of private or public customers.

The competing relations of the industry, another factor of local adaptation, are rather particular and are characterized by a situation of precarious and unstable balance among competitors of various sizes and origins. The margins are indeed very weak, and strong competition in a given area or county is immediately transformed into price wars and, in turn, negative margins. Thus, there is a balance between the competitors, as each one tries to preserve a certain number of specific customers. In any event, a plurality of supply is necessary: the local communities would not accept there being only one company for a given area. Nevertheless, this balance is fragile, and a contraction of demand encourages competitors to encroach on the field of the others. The companies are therefore involved in a downward spiral beginning with tiny profit margins, which then become negative. In this case, the least powerful companies are eliminated, the most fragile being most often the smallest. The large companies also suffer, however, laying off employees who will be the first to recreate small entities. It is thus very difficult to return to normal profitability when a zone has been affected in this way.

The subtlety of this competitive game, the marking of reserved territory by means of more or less formal signals, requires strong local involvement. Furthermore, it is important to have the possibility to react in the event of aggressive behavior on behalf of competitors: the reaction must be credible and, therefore, rapid. This involves the possibility of quickly modifying the objectives of profitability and the strategic choices.

Competitive advantage and mastery of the competitive game also involve strong involvement in the local networks. It is a question of establishing privileged bonds with local customers, which is worthwhile both at the level of the agency manager as well as that of the foreman. It is in particular a question of being able to play a real role of counsel, beyond responding to the invitation to tender. It is only this intimate knowledge of specificities of the local medium that can be used as a basis for decision-making. The local actors are the only ones who control it. This involvement in the local medium goes much further than the simple commercial approach: it is not a question of selling a product but of living on location in the field. For this reason, the large majority of the centers' personnel are recruited in the area. The agency managers and the foremen must even be notable locals, maintaining their role by participating in the collective life of the community (by belonging to the Rotary Club, for example).

The need for local adaptation is reinforced by a technical constraint. The materials used are not very expensive, and the costs of transportation quickly become very significant. The operating range of a production unit is thus very limited: a circle with a maximum diameter of 120 kilometers. Beyond this distance, the company can no longer be competitive, and the best supply will be that of the company nearest to the proposed construction site. Therefore, all levels of the vertical value chain can be found on site: from the production of raw materials (quarries) to the realization of the end product (on the construction site) and including the project study. In addition, it is impossible to standardize production. Indeed, the products must be adapted to the raw materials and local conditions; there is thus always a portion of the development which must be carried out locally.

In addition, the profession is governed by the procedure of invitations to tender and by the budgetary constraints of the local communities. The local communities are largely dependent upon the State's budget, and as a consequence it is difficult to precisely predict if such and such a project will indeed take place before the promulgation of a finance act. In the same way, the procedure of the invitation to tender, for both public and private clients, always leaves a great uncertainty in the renewal of contracts for the following year. Generally, the order book seldom exceeds three or four months (it can even be reduced to about fifteen days). To these can be added the constraints related to weather conditions: at the most basic level, activity depends on rain and good weather. Only the agency managers and his collaborators can evaluate, thanks to their knowledge of the market and probabilistic logic, the foreseeable volume of business for the period to come. These considerable constraints of local adaptation contrast with a marked need for integration.

The margin realized on the construction sites is relatively small. A particularly rigorous management is thus necessary in order to maintain a positive margin. Tools of management control which allow for a continuous follow-up of activity in all of its details must be introduced. It is also a question of being able to follow the profitability of the construction site from day to day, optimizing equipment flows and comprehensively using the financial resources. The data-processing tools necessary for this follow-up are generally too cumbersome to be locally developed or make a profit. Furthermore, the local actors feel less involved by this type of global concern.

Research and development constitute one of the essential assets of the company. Developing new surface coating that increase draining, reduce noise, or can be colored, allows for a certain differentiation. Thus, by means of the variants in the invitations to tender, the company that has an innovative product can win the bid in the context of strong competition characteristic of certain geographical sectors. Colas has a central laboratory which groups together 30 people, giving it a considerable capacity for innovation at the agency level.

The difficulty of giving a detailed forecast of activity for each peripheral unit implies being able to support a non-profitable sub-unit for a relatively long period of time. This maintenance is necessary for permanence and long-term profitability: the threat of response in the event of competitive confrontation must be credible and the non-profitable sectors should not be abandoned. Only by belonging to the group can the peripheral unit's survival be guaranteed. It is remarkable to note that activity is unpredictable only at the level of the peripheral unit: at the group level, the cyclical variations of the economic situation are offset, and profitability is satisfactory and foreseeable.

GTIE

GTIE is the French leader in electrical installation. In 2002, the group had a turnover of 3 billion Euros for a consolidated result of 79 million Euros. It employs 26 000 people. 31% of the turnover is realized out of France.

Telecommunications account for 10% of the turnover, 45% for industry, 25% for services and 20% for energy and infrastructures.

Group GTIE constitutes the electrical installation subsidiary of the Vinci group, which is principal shareholder. The role played by Vinci is little different than that of a stockholder, with certain transactions within the group being facilitated, however. Let us note that Vinci previously controlled other companies that were in competition with GTIE. A recent reorganization made it possible to link these entities to GTIE.[31] Their organization, specific within Vinci, was preserved and applied to the recently integrated structures. The organization which we describe has thus been reinforced and made permanent.

Principal Strategic Elements

The origin of the group's activity is electrical installation. Traditionally, for the building of a factory, a project-managing company would consult companies like GTIE, starting from pre-established plans. The activity was primarily labor-intensive. Recent developments have been moving towards more complete services, including carrying out studies and, if possible, sharing the engineering that has particularly technical elements. It is about being able to integrate automated elements and handle the processing of information. Maintenance is also an element to be controlled.

There are essentially three fields in which the group intervenes: the infrastructures (primarily public clients), the tertiary sector (equipment for all types of buildings) and industry (optimization of production). The fields of application are varied, but the activities are similar, the connection being that of intervention 'on all the levels of the electric chain'.

The first axis of the group's development consists in integrating the elements of information processing and communication to its supply in all sectors. The second axis of development relates to a particular target, that of the local communities that delegate an increasingly large part of their services. The third axis of development is internationalization, more particularly that directed towards Europe and Southeast Asia.

The Group's Structure[32]

The group is the result of the merger of three distinct entities: Mors Jean Bouchon, Garczynski and Traploir, and Fournié-Gropaud, each entity was more specifically present in corresponding parts of the French territory. The

31. In February 2003, GTIE changed its name to become Vinci Energy.
32. The structure is described here before the integration of the Vinci group's electrical activity.

organization adopted after the consolidation is centered around three 'poles of management' which bear the names of the original entities, except for Mors Jean Bouchon that has been renamed GTIE. However, divisions between these poles of management do not scrupulously follow the financial organizational chart. The logic behind its regrouping, interweaving geographical and industrial criteria, imposed a division that was different from the original.

The general management of the group is composed of the CEOs of the three groups, who remain legally independent of GTIE's general manager. Then, for each pole, the management committee assembles the chairman of each pole, one or more general managers or associate general managers, an 'administrative and financial' director or 'financial and accounting' director and a certain number of regional directors. The only functional supports, apart from financial, are a marketing director and a technical and commercial development director for GTIE. The regional managers are in charge of a certain number of 'companies' (the name used by GTIE to designate operational sub-units); they thus constitute an intermediate level of management between the center and the peripheral units and coordinate the activity for a zone or a given trade. The organization chart of the group is presented in Figure A.5.

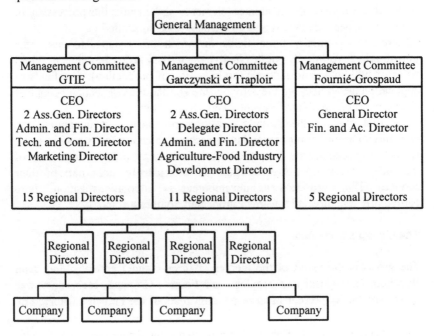

Figure A.5. Structure of GTIE Group

Structure of the Peripheral Units

The group is composed of 250 'companies'[33] which constitute the basic peripheral units. As at the preceding level, it is not the legal firm structures that makes it possible to distinguish between the 'companies': some are subsidiary companies, but there are subsidiary companies which include several 'companies' (in this case, they can share the administrative portion). The 'companies' comprise between 15 and 150 people and can intervene in engineering projects, in engineering projects associated with construction or in construction only. Their size is not dependent upon their activity: certain engineering units can comprise up to 120 people.

The structures of the 'companies' are very varied; however, there are certain common elements. First, the company director: he is the only one to have a hierarchical relationship with the other employees. The life of the 'company' is then organized around a certain number of projects. A particularly significant group of agents is that of the account managers who handle the complete follow-up on a contract, from pricing to after-sales. The account manager is the principal contact person for the customer. When a business is launched, a project manager is also named for the technical aspects, which may or may not be the account manager. In all cases, there is no real department composed and each project draws from all of the 'company's' resources. An ad hoc team is thus put together for each project, as no team is ever fixed. Administrative matters can be handled by a cell shared either by two companies or directly by the company.

Analysis of the Context

In all of GTIE's activities, the relational aspect is of primary importance. Response time, as well as the quality of relationships, plays a significant role in getting contracts from not only public clients but also from private ones. It is important to accompany one's clients, to be able to detect new needs on the basis of existing transactions. Furthermore, there is generally a limited time horizon for decisions that have to be made very quickly. Long-term detailed planning is therefore difficult: one must be able to react very quickly to a client's demands.

This is reinforced by the fact that GTIE's activity only deals with customized projects. The projects also vary in size, requiring that local structures have a strong capacity of readjustment and that the teams be able to constantly reorganize themselves in order to respond to a particular request.

---

33. Recent developments have increased the number of companies to 700, counting the elements coming from Vinci and new acquisitions. However, as we have emphasized, the organization that we have described was the one adopted.

The non-standardization of operation and the need for constant adaptation and flexibility fully justify a structure with strong autonomy.

Moreover, the group must be able to offer integrated services, from basic electricity to automation and even to the maintenance of the installations that have been carried out. These services are ensured for clients from various sectors, mobilizing different skills in different ways. These multiple skills mean integrating individuals who do very different things but who can be brought together to work. The strong autonomy allowed on site makes it easy to have the necessary skills available.

Beyond these points that require great autonomy within the group, certain elements must be dealt with centrally. The activities are users of innovation: they must integrate multiple technologies.

The central structure has a double role of vigilance and reflection concerning new technologies to integrate and possible new departments. These elements are particularly significant if one takes into account the group's desire to include information processing in its supply. In this field, expensive software can be purchased by the center and used by several peripheral units. This activity of vigilance and buying goes beyond what one small, isolated company could do alone.

The group is also an asset with respect to each company's clients. At the same time, it represents a commercial asset and the guarantee of a certain permanence. The companies must thus be able to display the fact that they belong to GTIE. For certain clients, it is necessary to call in a director to emphasize the fact that the response to an offer emanates from a group and not from a regrouping of SMEs. The companies demonstrate increased solidarity compared to the image generated by the group: they need the institution in order to develop and affirm themselves with respect to their competitors.

In addition, the companies can only develop skills available within the group by carrying out joint projects. One of the competing assets of GTIE is indeed its polyvalence in the field of electric integration. Very often, it is difficult for an isolated managing director to find the right partner within the group to formulate a common response to the expectations of the client. The central structures of the group then play a very important role of 'facilitator' for the implementation of a network logic. They make it possible for the various managers of the companies to meet, because the directors are more and more able to give indications about the right contacts for a particular project.

Appendix II
Summary of methodology

This work is the fruit of a long research task undertaken within the framework of a doctoral thesis at Paris-Dauphine University. It is thus based on a very solid methodology whose principal elements are presented in this appendix.

The general structure of this research arises from the need for meeting a double requirement: to take into account already existing research on the topic and to look further into the topic by carrying out a detailed assessment of the evolution of the companies studied. It was necessary to put together new knowledge on the basis of the conceptual framework described in the first chapter. In order to do this, our research called upon the well-known process using multiple and imbedded case studies. Four companies were selected out of the six that were originally considered: Air Liquide, CFDP, Colas and GTIE. Within these companies, several units were studied in detail.

It was important to have a good understanding of the operation of the four companies studied and to analyze them in detail. The methodology used thus aims to seize both general elements of the structures and more precise elements of the relations between individuals. It must also allow for an intensive and extensive description of the studied phenomenon. To meet these requirements, we adopted a mixed approach comprising both qualitative and quantitative elements.

A MIXED APPROACH

Case studies are often associated with a qualitative approach. However, they are not confined to this and can even adopt a completely quantitative approach. There are in fact many synergies between the two approaches: the use of quantitative information can highlight non-obvious relations to the researcher or can reinforce the convictions acquired by the qualitative approach; qualitative data makes it possible to interpret the results obtained in a quantitative manner.

Qualitative data aims to acquire intensive information starting from a restricted number of interviewees. They relate either to individual aspects concerning these interviewees or to aspects concerning the whole of the organization or an organizational sub-unit. They are collected by means of in-depth interviewing of a certain number of key informants and they allow for thorough comprehension of the relations existing within a unit or company and of the way cohesion is perceived by these actors.

In order to have an overall idea of the structures underlying the companies studied, especially at the inter-individual level, the interviews were supplemented by another approach: social networks analysis. The quantitative data that we collected relates to these inter-individual aspects. In each case, they were obtained by means of sociometric questionnaires used within one or several peripheral units. These questionnaires have allowed us to analyze the internal structure of the unit and to account for the relations the studied unit's agents maintain with the other units of the group and with external agents. This way one can study the nature of the social bonds which are at the root of the cohesion of the organization concerned. The data makes it possible to have extensive information which concerns a higher number of individuals. This is data that is complementary to that collected during the interviews.

The two approaches are complementary and enrich one another, making it possible to gain more complete and more varied experience on the case studies. The following example makes it possible to better understand the interest of combining the two methods. An individual belonging to peripheral unit A can be involved in an activity requiring frequent exchanges with unit B. He can, during an interview, recount many anecdotes showing his proximity and the frequency of the relations he maintains with the individuals of unit B. The interview only informs us of the relations of the individual questioned. What about the bonds/relations between the other individuals that have a similar position in the unit? Analyzing the social networks makes it possible to give a response for all the individuals of a unit. However, the questionnaires can only be really interpreted when one also has access to the wealth of qualitative information that comes from the interview.

THE SOURCES OF EVIDENCE

The mixed nature of the data selected directly implies an increased effort of triangulation. Triangulation consists of crossing the sources of data. The concern of the researcher must compare new information coming from one source with another source of data.

Without necessarily wanting to collect 'good points' for the accumulation of these sources, it seems natural to want to use all of the relevant sources. Thus, we used elements of documentation and archives, interviews, direct observation, and questionnaires.

Concerning documentation, the administrative documents were systematically collected, in particular those referring to the preparation of the annual budgets. Letters or 'memos' on precise subjects were also collected. Archives were less useful to us. However, aside from practical documents like the personnel files, annual reports and company newspapers and journals were systematically perused. Our presence was often necessary on site to lead the interviews, and we systematically sought to increase opportunities for direct observation: we asked to attend significant meetings of the studied units or to visit installations, buildings, etc.

Two essential sources nevertheless remain primary sources: the interviews and the questionnaires, which enabled us to collect the greatest quantity of information in direct relationship to the topic that interested us.

NATURE OF THE COLLECTED DATA

Topics of the Interviews

In order to guide the collection of data, it is necessary to shed light on the principal mechanisms by which the organizational modes contribute to the cohesion of the organization. These mechanisms and their uses are indicators of the contribution of each organizational mode to organizational cohesion. Table A.1 summarizes the operationalization of the conceptual framework in an interview grid.

What Networks to Study?

Two networks were analyzed with the goal of better determining to what extent a bureaucratic approach existed in the two companies. The network of control takes an interest in *ex post* control. The network of influence refers to *ex ante* control and to behavior modification. The other three relations are more likely to include cooperative mechanisms: the networks of contact, advice/aid and trust. The set of studied networks makes it possible to accurately represent the nature of the relations between peripheral units and those between the center and the periphery.

It now remains for us to delineate the questions that were posed. It was indeed necessary to collect information on the relations that the agents of the units studied maintained, on the one hand, with the agents of the other units

Table A.1 Operationalization of the conceptual framework

MODE OF ORGANIZATION	MECHANISMS	MAIN REFERENCES
The Market	• Internal competition • Extent of competing activities • Intensity of competition • Transfers between units • Importance of transactions • Type of delivery price used • Sharing of profits and variable remuneration • Foundation of variable remuneration • Internalization of the goals by the actors	Lebas and Weigenstein (1986)
The Bureaucracy	• Input control • Direct influence exerted on the periphery's choices • Coordination of activities between peripheral units • Allocation of resources • Output control • Nature of objectives to be reached • Process of determining objectives • Breakdown of follow-up procedures • Pressure and systems of incentive	Goold and Campbell (1987)
The Clan	• Recruitment • Career development • Training • Organizational vision and values	De Woot and Maredsans (1984)
The Network	• Sharing of resources • Carrying out of common projects • Transfer of competences/skills • Collegiality in decision-making	Bahrami (1992), Waters (1989)

of the company and, on the other hand, with the agents external to the company. A first series of questions for each network studied relates to the internal relations of the unit. In this case, individuals can be identified. Two other series of questions correspond to the relations which individuals maintain with the other units of the group and with the external entities as a whole (i.e. one does not identify by name the people with whom the studied peripheral agents are in contact outside their unit). It is thus possible to conceive the internal network of each peripheral unit studied as a network open to an internal environment (the rest of the organization) and to an external environment. This choice thus yields a satisfactory compromise for research on inter-unit cohesion.

CHOOSING THE CASES

With the type of data to be collected on each case fixed, it was then necessary for us to determine how many cases the study must include and then choose the companies to be studied. The number of cases was not determined in advance, as the original idea was to choose several cases with similar approaches to center-periphery and periphery-periphery relationships. We sought out companies which particularly stressed the importance of granting autonomy to the peripheral units or an idea of decentralization. The idea of cross-cutting activities was a second criterion which could be expressed in various forms, for example 'horizontal communication', 'knitting', 'networks', etc. It was particularly difficult to determine before a few interviews the contribution of each case, and thus several cases were considered and later ruled out. A communications company got our attention from the very beginning. It turned out that, following the first interviews, center-periphery relations were more marked by the control of results that by operation in network. At the same time, a transport company interested us because it comprised a unit of non-hierarchical coordination within a group of peripheral units which themselves had increased autonomy. However, we quickly realized that the unit in question actually had real power of injunction and that autonomy was very measured.

Having originally envisaged studying six cases, we thus had four cases that corresponded to our problematic. We did not expect that a single company would allow us to point out all the possibilities offered by the network as an organizational mode. However, the only basis we had at the beginning of this research project was insights on the various types of complementarities between sub-units on which the network organizational mode could be based. It was then a question of finding cases which corresponded to a specialization that was different from the members of the network (i.e. the sub-units): geographical specialization, specialization by both vertically and horizontally complementary trades. The four cases selected made it possible to cover all of the complementarities considered (see Table A.2).

Another significant element for the selection process was the idea that two companies could handle a similar situation of complementarity between the peripheral units in different manners. The network is not the only possibility for organizing, and each company studied is confronted with an arbitration between the organizational modes. It is this second criterion of selection which encouraged us to retain two cases that have the exclusive characteristic of geographical complementarity of the operational sub-units.

Table A.2 Specialization of the peripheral units

CASE STUDIES	TYPE OF COMPLEMENTARITY BETWEEN THE MEMBERS
Air Liquide	• Vertical • Horizontal geographics
CFDP	• Horizontal geographics
Colas	• Horizontal geographics
GTIE	• Horizontal by trade • Vertical

DATA COLLECTION AND PROCESSING

For each case, via our contact with the company, we determined the units where a thorough analysis could be conducted – they were the units where several series of interviews were carried out and where sociometric questionnaires were done. The selection of the units forms an integral part of the process of the embedded case study design. We retained, depending on which case, two or three units. The selected criterion was that of the 'representativeness' of the units selected. Whatever the structure involved, there were less typical units, exerting their activity in related trades or in particular fields. These more exceptional cases were generally separate from the in-depth study. However, we did meet the directors of these marginal units or one central informant who knew them well. Table A.3 summarizes the units studied for each case.

Table A.3 Peripheral units studied for each case

CASES	UNITS STUDIED	TRADE
Colas	• Two agencies	• Geographical units (road resurfacing)
CFDP	• Three teams	• Units of representation
GTIE	• Two companies	• Processing of geographical information • Manufacturing of electrical equipment boxes
L'Air Liquide	• Two regions • National establishment	• Customer service center • Production establishment

Qualitative Data Collection and Processing

In addition to certain elements coming from the secondary data and direct observation, the richest of the qualitative data comes from the interviews carried out in the field. They are one- to four-hour semi-directive interviews (interviews or conversations of shorter length are not listed). The topics of reference arise from the conceptual framework. The questions thus concern the four organization modes and the way in which they can be activated within the company. The interview grid is used to start a dialogue; these topics are supplemented by more general questions about the bonds maintained by the interviewees with the other units of the company.

Table A.4 presents the series of interviews (at least one hour long) that were carried out in the four companies studied; many meetings or shorter exchanges were not indexed. Our concern was to collect from points of view that were as varied as possible by conducting interviews at all hierarchical levels. On the one hand, it was a question of avoiding superficial speech with which we were sometimes confronted from wary/suspicious interviewees; on the other hand, the actors' representations on various levels generally brought about different enlightening information on the studied topics.

The analysis of the qualitative data can be broken down into two phases: first, the analysis carried out during the collection of the data and, second, the analysis carried out for the drafting of the final document. It seemed necessary to systematically carry out an analysis during the data-gathering.

The on-site notes and interview transcripts were systematically formatted in the days following the interview. We then drew up a case summary form. The notes were divided into small numbered paragraphs of sets of themes and, on the form, there was the topic that the paragraph dealt with. We then briefly noted the questions that were well dealt with by the interview and those remaining that were left 'in suspense' and thus had to be approached in another interview. This categorization made it possible at the same time to prepare the data for the final analysis and to focus the data collection for the following interviews. The final analysis of the cases was greatly facilitated by the work carried out during data-gathering. Qualitative analysis of the functioning of each of the organizations' structures was made while trying to remain as close as possible to the data collected from the interviews.

Table A.4 List of series of interviews carried out

AIR LIQUIDE	N	CFDP*	N	COLAS	N	GTIE	N
• National Management	5	• Region/ national	9	• National management	7	• Central management	3
• Support units	2	• Region	2	• Regional management	9		
• Regions	18	• Functional units	2	• Agencies	9	• Companies	11
• Production establishment	5						

Note: *As CFDP is a collegial structure, many delegates have both a local and national role within the company.

Collection and Processing of Quantitative Data

Data is collected by means of 'name generators' (i.e. questions relating to the individuals with whom the interviewee has a relationship). While being inspired by prior research and by adapting this research to our own objectives, we retained the following questions for the five networks that interest us:

1. Direct contact for work: Who are the people with whom you are in frequent contact within the framework of your work?

2. Control: Who are the people that exert direct or indirect control over the result and/or quality of the work that you carry out? Who are the people over whose result and /or quality of work you exert direct or indirect control?
3. Influence: Who are the people whose declarations, suggestions or judgments, whether in general or on a specific point, change the way in which you act? Who are the people whose ways of acting you think of modifying by your declarations, suggestions or judgments whether in general or on a specific point?
4. Advice/help: Who are the people who advise you or who come to your assistance on specific points? Who are the people you advise or to whose assistance you come on specific points?
5. Trust: Who are the people you particularly trust to speak with about touchy professional problems?

These questions were asked in a very broad manner. Indeed, during the administration of a test questionnaire, certain people refused to answer more direct questions, those including the word *influence* for example.

Three of the networks studied are oriented networks and involved posing two series of questions per network: networks of control, of influence, and of advice/help. Indeed, the two questions allowed us to make crosschecks between the individuals' declarations: if A claims to exert some control over B, does B indicate that he or she is being controlled by A? They also made it possible to easily deal with the rare problems of missing individuals. The network of contact not being oriented (if A is in contact with B, then B is in contact with A), only one question asked of the two individuals was sufficient. The network of trust is oriented by nature, however, crosschecks are useless here (if A trusts B, it does not seem useful to ask B if he thinks that A trusts him).

The questions selected were pre-tested on eight people before posing them to Colas, the first company concerned. They were then tested again in the company itself on five people at various levels. The tests were carried out by directly administrating the questionnaire and by requiring that the person questioned share his thoughts little by little as he was writing them. After some trials, the questionnaire was accepted without need for modification and we thus decided to launch the test at Colas. In order to facilitate the answers, three lists were drawn up. The first list comprises the names of the internal people of the unit; the second list indexes the other entities of the company; the third list relates to the organizations outside the company. These lists were made up during discussions with people of the peripheral unit up until the point that no element was added by the last person with whom we met.

The sociometric questionnaires drawn up in this way made it possible to get individual data gathered in various ways in order to analyze the structure at different levels. Each network (contact, control, influence, help/advice, trust) was analyzed successively to help produce a summary about all of the networks. This part explains in detail the three analyses on which rests our thought on inter-individual structures: an analysis of the opening of the unit measured by an overall indicator, an analysis of gatekeepers, and an analysis of the joint activity between internal and external networks. These three analyses were carried out for each network concerned.

The analysis of the overall opening of the units to the exterior is based on a principal indicator: the number of people in a unit who have relations with the various categories of external entities (central unit of the company, other peripheral units, and entities outside the group). This first indicator helps us evaluate whether overall the actors of a peripheral unit maintain links for the network concerned with categories of agents that do not belong to the unit. For each category of actors, one then analyzes the openness of the unit in more detail. For example, external agents will be broken down into customers, suppliers, competitors, etc.; the result of this analysis is essential within the framework of our research. It indeed brings invaluable information on the nature of the relations between center and periphery, between periphery and periphery as well as between the periphery and external agents.

The second analysis uses the concept of marginal gatekeeper. The gatekeeper is an individual who has a certain margin of autonomy because he belongs to several relational universes. Gatekeepers play the role of guard of the organizational border and it is through their intervention that information between the interior and the outside of a unit passes. Individual aspects not being at the heart of our concerns, we prefer to analyze the role of gate-keepers by type of position. For each network we have thus highlighted the types of positions which are at the origin of the opening of the organizational border. Individual exceptions are also of course important and they were taken into account. This analysis thus makes it possible to understand which agents are the ones carrying out organizational cohesion; it goes beyond the analysis of openness and looks at inter-individual structures.

The third analysis seeks to highlight the joint activity between the internal structure of the unit and of the external structure. The idea here is that the network does not stop at the organizational border. Various means of processing can be carried out on the internal data: by analyzing the matrices of sociometric data, calculating the scores of centrality, and searching for cliques.

First of all, the data is all gathered in the form of matrices that indicate the relations between individuals. These matrices are then processed to eliminate non-symmetry from the data. For example, in the case of the network of control, we ask each individual a question about the people whose activities he or she controls and about the people who control his or her activity. If A indicates that he or she exerts control over B and B did not mention it in the list of the people who control him or her, then the link between A and B will not be taken into account. Such reasoning applies to all of the networks, with the exception of the network of trust. The rule is thus to eliminate any data not confirmed by the two individuals.

This matricial data makes it possible to calculate scores of centrality and intermediarity for each individual. The individuals having a high score of centrality or intermediarity play a significant role in the network concerned. We seek to isolate the individuals having a score higher than average (average corrected by eliminating the extreme values). Analysis of the internal network comes from the need for better understanding the operation of the unit studied. It is important to explain the genesis of organizational cohesion.

The third part of the processing carried out is the search for cliques. A clique is a group of individuals that are all linked together in the network concerned. Cliques are a group of strong cohesion. The search for cliques thus helps identify internal sub-groups.

References

Argyris, C. (1991), 'Teaching smart people how to learn', *Harvard Business Review*, May-June, pp. 99-109.

Baden-Fuller, C. and Stopford, J. (1993), *Rejuvenating the Mature Business*, London: Routledge.

Bahrami, H. (1992), 'The emerging flexible organization: perspectives from Silicon Valley', *California Management Review*, summer, pp. 33-52.

Bartlett, C.A. and Ghoshal, S. (1989), *Managing Across Borders: the Transnational Solution*, Boston: Harvard Business School Press.

Block, Z. and MacMillan, I.C. (1993), *Corporate Venturing*, Boston: Harvard Business School Press.

Bradach, J.L. and Eccles, R.G. (1989), 'Price, authority, and trust: from ideal types to plural forms', *Annual Review of Sociology*, Palo Alto, 15, pp. 87-118.

Burgelman, R.A. (1983), Corporate entrepreneurship and strategic management: insights from a process study, *Management Science*, **29** (12), pp. 1349-65.

Chakravarthy, B. and Gargiulo, M. (1998), 'Maintaining leadership in the transition to new organizational forms', *Journal of Management Studies*, **35** (4), July, pp. 437-56.

Chiles, T.H. and McMackin, J.F. (1996), 'Integrating variable risk preferences, trust, and transaction cost economics', *Academy of Management Review*, **21** (1), pp. 73-99.

David, A. (1995), *RATP: la métamorphose, réalités et théorie du pilotage du changement*, Paris: Interéditions.

Day, D.L. (1994), 'Raising radicals: different processes for championing innovative corporate ventures', *Organization Science*, **5** (2), May, pp. 148-75.

De Woot, P. and de Maredsans, D.X. (1984), *Le management stratégique des groupes industriels: fonctionnement au sommet et culture d'entreprise*, Economica.

Denton, D.K. (1991), *Horizontal Management*, Lexington Books.

Doty, H., Glick, W.H. and Huber, C.P. (1993), 'fit, equifinality and organizational effectiveness: a test of two configurational theories', *Academy of Management Journal*, **36** (6), pp. 1196-250.

Eccles, R.G. and Crane, D.B. (1987), 'Managing through networks in investment banking', *California Management Review*, Fall, pp. 176-95.

Ezzamel, M., Lilley, S. and Willmott, W. (1994), 'The New organization and the New managerial work', *European Management Journal*, **21** (4), December, pp. 454-61.

Feneuille, S. (1990), 'A network organization to meet the challenges of complexity', *European Management Journal*, **8** (3), September, pp. 296-301.

Foss, N.J. (2002), 'New organizational forms – critical perspectives', *International Journal of the Economics of Business*, **9** (1), pp. 1-8.

Frost, T.S. (2001), 'The geographic sources of foreign subsidiaries' innovations', *Strategic Management Journal*, **22** (2), pp. 101-23.

Gabriel, Y. (1995), 'The unmanaged organization: stories, fantasies and subjectivity', *Organization Studies*, **16** (3), pp. 477-501.

Gennen, H. (1984), 'The case for managing by the numbers', *Fortune*, 1st October.

Ghoshal, S. and Moran, P. (1996), 'Bad for practice: a critique of transaction cost theory', *Academy of Management Review*, **21** (1), January, pp. 13-47.

Gomory, R.E. and Schmitt, R.W. (1991), 'Science et produit', *Revue Française de Gestion*, Juin-Juillet-Août.

Gooderham, P.N. and Ulset, S. (2002), 'Beyond the M-form: towards a critical test of the new form', *International Journal of the Economics of Business*, **9** (1), pp. 117-38.

Goold, M. and Campbell, A. (1987), *Strategies and Styles*, London: Blackwell.

Graham, M.A. and LeBaron, M.J. (1994), *'The Horizontal Revolution'*, Jossey-Bass Publishers.

Granovetter, M. (1985), 'Economic action and social structure: the problem of embeddedness', *American Journal of Sociology*, **91** (8), November, pp. 483-510.

Gupta, A.K. and Govindarajan, V. (2000), 'Knowledge management's social dimension: lessons from Nucor steel', *Sloan Management Review*, **42**, pp. 71-80.

Hamel, G. and Prahalad, C.K. (1989), 'Strategic intent', *Harvard Business Review*, May-June, pp. 63-76.

Hammer, M. and Champy, J. (1993), *Reengineering the Corporation*, New York: HarperCollins.

Handy, C. (1990), *The Age of Unreason*, Boston: Harvard Business School Press.

Hansen, M.T. (1999), 'The search-transfer problem: the role of weak ties in sharing knowledge across organization subunits', *Administration Science Quarterly*, **44** (1), pp. 82-111.

Hansen, M.T. (2002), 'Knowledge networks: explaining effective knowledge sharing in multiunit companies', *Organization Science*, **13** (1), May-June, pp. 232-48.

Hedlund, G. (1994), 'A model of knowledge management and the N-form corporation, *Strategic Management Journal*, **15**, pp. 454-61.

Hernes, T. (1999), 'Flexible learning systems and obsolete organization structures: steps towards bridging the gap', *Scandinavian Journal of Management*, **15**, pp. 89-110.

Imai, K. and Itami, H. (1984), 'Interpenetration of organization and market' *International Journal of Industrial Organization*, **2**, pp. 285-310.

Jarillo, J.C. (1988), 'On strategic networks', *Strategic Management Journal*, **9**, pp. 31-41.

Johanson, J. and Mattsson, L. (1992), 'Network positions and strategic action', in B. Axelsson and Easton (eds), *Industrial Networks, a New View of Reality*, Routledge.

Kogut, B. and Zander, U. (1992), 'Knowledge of the firm, combinative capabilities and the replication of technology', *Organization Science*, **3** (3), pp. 383-97.

Lazega, E. (1992), 'Analyse de réseaux d'une organisation collégiale : les avocats d'affaires', *Revue Française de Sociologie* **33**.

Lebas, M. and Weigenstein, J. (1986), 'Management control: the roles of rules, markets and culture', *Journal of Management Studies*, **23** (3), May, pp. 259-71.

Lenz, R.T. and Lyles, M. (1985), 'Paralysis by analysis: is your planning system becoming too rational?', *Long Range Planning*, **18**, August.

Lewin, A.Y. and Volberda, H.W. (1999), 'Prolegomena on coevolution: a framework for research on strategy and new organizational forms', *Organization Science*, **10** (5), September-October, pp. 519-34.

Markides, C.C. and Williamson, P.J. (1994), 'Related diversification, core competences and corporate performance', *Strategic Management Journal*, **15** (5), pp. 149-65.

Marmonier, L. and Thiétart, R.A. (1993), 'Les nouveaux problèmes de structure et de gestion des entreprises', *Cahiers de DMSP*, Université Paris-Dauphine, **220**, October.

Marx, T. (1991), 'Removing the obstacles to effective strategic planning', *Long Range Planning*, **24** (4), August, pp. 21-8.

Merali, Y. (2000), 'Individual and collective congruence in the knowledge management process', *Journal of Strategic Information Systems*, **9**, pp. 213-34.

Meyer, A.D., Tsui, A.S. and Hinings, C.R. (1993), 'Configurational approach to organizational analysis', *Academy of Management Review*, **36** (6), pp. 1175-95.

Midler, C. (1993), *L'auto qui n'existait pas, Management des projets et transformation de l'entreprise*, Paris: Interéditions.

Miles, R.E. and Snow, C.C. (1992), 'Managing 21st century network organizations', *Organizational Dynamics*, **20** (3), Winter, pp. 5-20.

Miles, R.E., Snow, C.C., Mathews, J.A., Miles, G. and Coleman, H.J. (1997), 'Organizing in the knowledge age: anticipating the cellular form', *Academy of Management Executive*, **11** (4), pp. 7-19.

Mintzberg, H. (1979), *The Structuring of Organizations: a Synthesis of the Research*, Prentice-Hall.

Mintzberg, H. (1980), 'Structure in 5s: a synthesis of the research on organization design', *Management Science*, **26** (3) March.

Mintzberg, H. (1981), 'Organization design: fashion or fit', *Harvard Business Review*, January-February.

Mintzberg, H. (1989), *Mintzberg on Management: Inside our Strange World of Organizations*, Free Press.

Mintzberg, H. (1993), 'The pitfalls of strategic planning', *California Management Review*, **36** (1), Fall, p. 47.

Mintzberg, H. (1994), *The Rise and Fall of Strategic Planning*, Prentice-Hall International.

Mintzberg, H. and Waters J.A. (1985), 'Of strategies, deliberate and emergent', *Strategic Management Journal*, **6**.

Morgan, G. (1986), *Images of Organization*, Sage Publications.

Nahapiet, J. and Ghoshal, S. (1998), 'Social capital, intellectual capital, and the organizational advantage', *Academy of Management Review*, **23** (2), pp. 242-66.

Nonaka, I. (1994), 'A dynamic theory of organizational knowledge creation', *Organization Science*, **5** (1), pp. 14-37.

Nonaka, I. and Takeuchi, H. (1994), *The Knowledge Creating Company*, New York: Oxford University Press.

Ostoroff, F. (1999), *The Horizontal Organization*, Oxford University Press.

Ouchi, W.G. (1979), 'A conceptual framework for the design of organizational control mechanisms', *Management Science*, **25** (9), September, pp. 833-48.

Ouchi, W.G. (1980), 'Markets, bureaucracies and clans', *Administrative Science Quarterly*, **25** (1), March, pp. 129-41.

Ouchi, W.G. and Jaeger, A.M. (1978), 'Type Z organization : stability in the midst of mobility', *Academy of Management Review*, **3** (2), April, pp. 305-14.

Powell, W. (1990), 'Neither markets, nor hierarchy, network form of organization', in Staw and Cummings (eds), *Research in Organization Behavior*, **12**, Greenwich, Conn.: Ji Press, pp. 295-336.

Quinn, J. B. (1992), *Intelligent Enterprise*, New York: Free Press.

Quinn Mills, D. and Friesen, B. (1992), 'The learning organization', *European Management Journal*, **10** (2), June, pp. 146-56.

Ravasi, D. and Verona, G. (2001), 'Organizing the process of knowledge integration: the benefits of structural ambiguity', *Scandinavian Journal of Management*, **17**, pp. 41-66.

Senge, P. (1990), 'The leader's new work: building learning organizations', *Sloan Management Review*, **32** (1), Fall, pp. 7-25.

Spencer, B.A. (1994), 'Models of organization and total quality management: a comparison and critical evaluation', *Academy of Management Review*, **19** (3), pp. 446-71.

Stalk, G. and Hout, T. (1990), *Competing Against Time: How Timebased Competition is Reshaping Global Markets*, New York: Free Press.

Thiétart, R.A. and Forgues, B. (1995), 'Chaos theory and organization', *Organization Science*, **6** (1), January-February, pp. 19-31.

Waters, M. (1989), 'Collegiality, bureaucratization and professsionalization: a Weberian analysis', *American Journal of Sociology*, **94** (5), March.

Wenger, E. (1999), *Communities of Practice: Learning, Meaning, and Identity*, Cambridge: Cambridge University Press.

Williamson, O.E. (1975), *Markets and Hierarchies: Analysis and Antitrust Implications*, New York: Free Press.

Williamson, O.E. (1985), *The Economic Institutions of Capitalism: Firms, Markets, Relational Contracting*, New York: Free Press.

Williamson, O.E. (1991), 'Comparative economic organization: the analysis of discrete structural alternatives', *Administrative Science Quarterly*, **36**, pp. 269-96.

Williamson, O.E. (1996), 'Economic organization: the case for candor', *Academy of Management Review*, **21** (1), pp. 48-57.

Winter, S.G. (1993), *On Coase, Competence, and the Corporation, The Nature of the Firm*, Oxford: Oxford University Press.

Zack, M.H., (1999), 'Managing codified knowledge', *Sloan Management Review*, **40**, Summer, pp. 45-58.

Zenger, T.R. (2002), 'Crafting internal hybrids: complementarities, common change initiatives, and the team-based organization', *International Journal of the Economics of Business*, **9** (1), pp. 79-95.

Name Index

Subject Index